YORK NOT

AQA ENGLISH LANGUAGE

PRACTICE TESTS WITH ANSWERS

SUSANNAH WHITE

PEARSON

 YORK PRESS

The right of Susannah White to be identified as the Author of this Work
has been asserted by her in accordance with the Copyright,
Designs and Patents Act 1988

YORK PRESS
322 Old Brompton Road, London SW5 9JH

PEARSON EDUCATION LIMITED
Edinburgh Gate, Harlow,
Essex CM20 2JE, United Kingdom
Associated companies, branches and representatives throughout the world

First published 2017

10 9 8 7 6 5

ISBN 978–1–2921–8633–7

Phototypeset by DTP Media
Printed in Slovakia

Photo credits: monkeybusinessimages/© iStock for page 6 bottom / David Vogt/
Shutterstock for page 17 middle / Ana Blazic Pavlovic/Shutterstock for page 22 top /
Alexander Kolomietz/Shutterstock for page 60 middle / Nataliia Melnychuk/Shutterstock
for page 65 top.

CONTENTS

PART ONE: INTRODUCTION

How to use these papers

This book contains four York Notes example GCSE English Language practice test papers: there are two Paper 1s (fiction) and two Paper 2s (non-fiction). All these York Notes papers have been modelled on the ones that you will sit in your AQA GCSE 9–1 English Language exams.

There are lots of ways these papers can support your study and revision for the AQA GCSE 9–1 English Language exam. There is no 'right' way – choose the one or ones that suits your learning style best.

You could use them:

1 **Alongside York Notes *AQA English Language and Literature: Revision and Exam Practice***

Do you have the York Notes *Revision and Exam Practice* guide for AQA GCSE English Language (and Literature)?

The papers in this book will allow you to try out the skills and techniques outlined in Chapters 1 to 6 of the guide. So you could:

● read a section of the guide dealing with one specific question type
● complete this question in one of the practice papers printed here.

2 **As a stand-alone revision programme**

Have you already mastered all of the skills needed for your exam?

Then you can keep your skills fresh by answering one or two questions from this book each day or week.

You could make a revision diary and allocate particular questions to particular times.

3 **As a form of mock exam**

Would you like to work under exam conditions?

You could put aside part of a day to work on a full paper in a quiet room. Set a stopwatch so that you can experience what it will be like in your real exam. If some of your friends have copies of this book then several of you could all do this together and discuss your answers afterwards.

4 **As a combination of revision and exam practice**

Would you like to do some revision and then try a mock exam?

Perhaps you could work through one set of papers slowly – question by question over a number of days – and then save the other set of papers to use as a mock nearer the exam.

How to use the answer sections

This book contains answer sections that will help you to understand what the examiners are looking for, and how your own responses compare against sample answers at a range of levels.

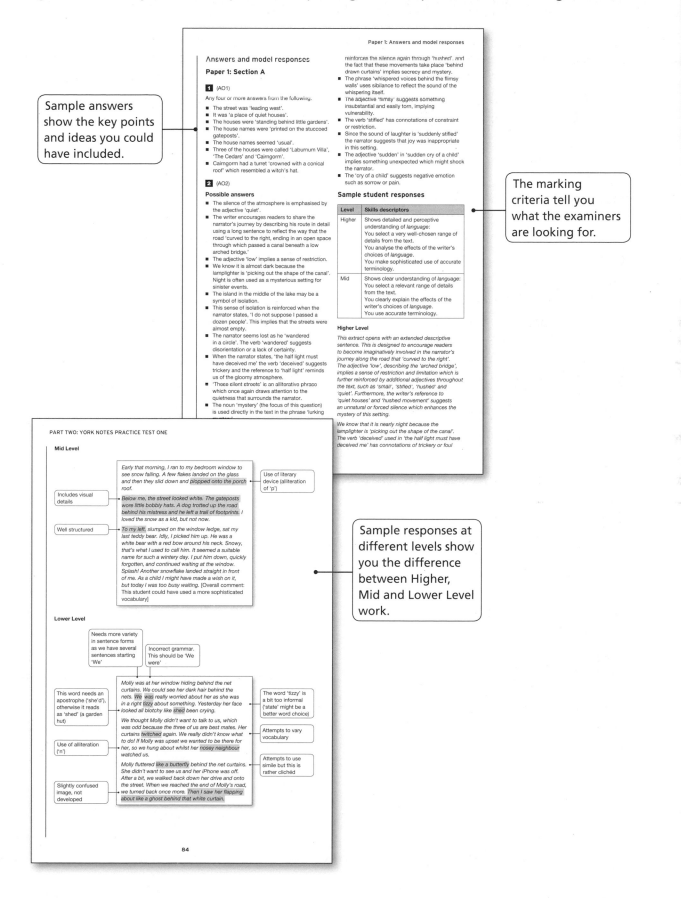

Sample answers show the key points and ideas you could have included.

The marking criteria tell you what the examiners are looking for.

Sample responses at different levels show you the difference between Higher, Mid and Lower Level work.

Assessment Objectives

Your work will be examined through the six Assessment Objectives (AOs) listed below. Each question in the practice papers is assessed by one or occasionally two of these.

Section A: Reading – Assessment Objectives

AO1	• Identify and interpret explicit and implicit information and ideas. • Select and synthesise evidence from different texts.
AO2	• Explain, comment on and analyse how writers use language and structure to achieve effects and influence readers, using relevant subject terminology to support their views.
AO3	• Compare writers' ideas and perspectives, as well as how these are conveyed, across two or more texts.
AO4	• Evaluate texts critically and support this with appropriate textual references.

Section B: Writing – Assessment Objectives

AO5	• Communicate clearly, effectively and imaginatively, selecting and adapting tone, style and register for different forms, purposes and audiences. • Organise information and ideas, using structural and grammatical features to support coherence and cohesion of texts.
AO6	• Use a range of vocabulary and sentence structures for clarity, purpose and effect, with accurate spelling and punctuation (20% of total marks).

AO coverage across the papers

The grids below show you the Assessment Objectives examined on each practice paper. As you can see, some AOs apply to both papers while others apply to only one paper. As you answer the questions in this book, keep checking these Assessment Objectives until you are sure which ones apply to each question. Then you will know exactly what the examiners are looking for.

Remember to notice the number of marks allowed for each question as this will help you to gauge how much you should write and how much time you should spend on each question.

Paper 1: Explorations in creative reading and writing

Section	Question number	AO	Number of marks
A	1	AO1	4
A	2	AO2	8
A	3	AO2	8
A	4	AO4	20
B	5	AO5, AO6	40

Paper 2: Writers' viewpoints and perspectives

Section	Question number	AO	Number of marks
A	1	AO1	4
A	2	AO1	8
A	3	AO2	12
A	4	AO3	16
B	5	AO5, AO6	40

PART TWO: YORK NOTES PRACTICE TEST ONE

Paper 1: Explorations in creative reading and writing

Time allowed: 1 hour 45 minutes

Materials

For this paper you must have:
- Source A – printed within the question paper.

Instructions

- Answer all questions.
- Answer the questions in the space provided, continuing onto a separate sheet if needed.
- Do all rough work in a notebook or on separate sheets of paper.
- You must refer to the sources provided.
- You should not use a dictionary.

Information

- The marks for questions are shown in brackets.
- The maximum mark for this paper is 80.
- There are 40 marks for Section A and 40 marks for Section B.
- You are reminded of the need for good English and clear presentation in your answers.
- The quality of your reading is assessed in Section A.
- The quality of your writing is assessed in Section B.

Advice

- You are advised to spend about 15 minutes reading through the source and all five questions you have to answer.
- You should make sure you leave sufficient time to check your answers.

Source A

This extract is taken from a Sherlock Holmes crime novel called *The Hound of the Baskervilles* by Sir Arthur Conan Doyle. This book was first published in serial form in 1901–2. In this extract Holmes and Watson hear a terrible sound on the moors.

Holmes had sprung to his feet, and I saw his dark, athletic outline at the door of the hut, his shoulders stooping, his head thrust forward, his face peering into the darkness.

'Hush!' he whispered. 'Hush!'

5 The cry had been loud on account of its vehemence, but it had pealed out from somewhere far off on the shadowy plain. Now it burst upon our ears, nearer, louder, more urgent than before.

'Where is it?' Holmes whispered; and I knew from the thrill of his voice that he, the man of iron, was shaken to the soul. 'Where is it, Watson?'

'There, I think.' I pointed into the darkness.

10 'No, there!'

Again the agonized cry swept through the silent night, louder and much nearer than ever. And a new sound mingled with it, a deep, muttered rumble, musical and yet menacing, rising and falling like the low, constant murmur of the sea.

'The hound!' cried Holmes. 'Come, Watson, come! Great heavens, if we are too late!'

15 He had started running swiftly over the moor, and I had followed at his heels. But now from somewhere among the broken ground immediately in front of us there came one last despairing yell, and then a dull, heavy thud. We halted and listened. Not another sound broke the heavy silence of the windless night.

I saw Holmes put his hand to his forehead like a man distracted.[1] He stamped his feet upon
20 the ground.

'He has beaten us, Watson. We are too late.'

'No, no, surely not!'

'Fool that I was to hold my hand.[2] And you, Watson, see what comes of abandoning your charge! But, by Heaven, if the worst has happened we'll avenge him!'

25 Blindly we ran through the gloom, blundering against boulders, forcing our way through gorse bushes, panting up hills and rushing down slopes, heading always in the direction whence those dreadful sounds had come. At every rise Holmes looked eagerly round him, but the shadows were thick upon the moor, and nothing moved upon its dreary face.

'Can you see anything?'

30 'Nothing.'

'But, hark, what is that?'

A low moan had fallen upon our ears. There it was again upon our left! On that side a ridge of rocks ended in a sheer cliff which overlooked a stone-strewn slope. On its jagged face was spread-eagled some dark, irregular object. As we ran towards it the vague outline hardened
35 into a definite shape. It was a prostrate man face downward upon the ground, the head doubled under him at a horrible angle, the shoulders rounded and the body hunched together as if in the act of throwing a somersault. So grotesque was the attitude that I could not for the instant realize that that moan had been the passing of his soul. Not a whisper, not a rustle, rose now from the dark figure over which we stooped. Holmes laid his hand upon
40 him and held it up again, with an exclamation of horror. The gleam of the match which he struck shone upon his clotted fingers and upon the ghastly pool which widened slowly from the crushed skull of the victim. And it shone upon something else which turned our hearts sick and faint within us – the body of Sir Henry Baskerville!

There was no chance of either of us forgetting that peculiar ruddy tweed suit – the very one
45 which he had worn on the first morning that we had seen him in Baker Street. We caught the one clear glimpse of it, and then the match flickered and went out, even as the hope had gone out of our souls. Holmes groaned, and his face glimmered white through the darkness.

'The brute! the brute!' I cried with clenched hands. 'Oh Holmes, I shall never forgive myself for having left him to his fate.'

___

Glossary

distracted[1] – mentally confused or deeply troubled by grief and anxiety.
hold my hand[2] – wait without taking action.

Turn over for Section A

Section A: Reading

Answer **all** questions in this section.
You are advised to spend about 45 minutes on this section.

1 Read again the first part of the source, **lines 1 to 13**.

List **four** things from this part of the text about the sound the two men hear.

[4 marks]

1 _____

_____

2 _____

_____

3 _____

_____

4 _____

_____

2 Look in detail at this extract from **lines 14 to 28** of the source:

'The hound!' cried Holmes. 'Come, Watson, come! Great heavens, if we are too late!'

He had started running swiftly over the moor, and I had followed at his heels. But now from somewhere among the broken ground immediately in front of us there came one last despairing yell, and then a dull, heavy thud. We halted and listened. Not another sound broke the heavy silence of the windless night.

I saw Holmes put his hand to his forehead like a man distracted. He stamped his feet upon the ground.

'He has beaten us, Watson. We are too late.'

'No, no, surely not!'

'Fool that I was to hold my hand. And you, Watson, see what comes of abandoning your charge! But, by Heaven, if the worst has happened we'll avenge him!'

Blindly we ran through the gloom, blundering against boulders, forcing our way through gorse bushes, panting up hills and rushing down slopes, heading always in the direction whence those dreadful sounds had come. At every rise Holmes looked eagerly round him, but the shadows were thick upon the moor, and nothing moved upon its dreary face.

How does the writer use language here to convey Holmes's desperation?

You could include the writer's choice of:

- words and phrases
- language features and techniques
- sentence forms.

[8 marks]

3 You now need to think about the **whole** of the **source.**

This text is taken from a chapter near the end of the novel *The Hound of the Baskervilles*.

How has the writer structured the text to interest you as a reader?

You could write about:

■ what the writer focuses your attention on at the beginning of the source
■ how and why the writer changes this focus as the source develops
■ any other structural features that interest you.

[8 marks]

_____

_____

_____

_____

_____

_____

_____

_____

_____

_____

_____

_____

_____

_____

_____

_____

_____

_____

_____

_____

_____

_____

4 Focus this part of your answer on the last part of the source, **from line 29 to the end.**

A student, having read this section of the text, said: 'The writer makes the moment when Holmes and Watson find the body very dramatic. I can feel the tension rising as I read it'.

To what extent do you agree?

In your response, you could:

■ write about your own impressions of the discovery of the body
■ evaluate how the writer has created these impressions
■ support your opinions with references to the text.

[20 marks]

_____

_____

_____

_____

_____

_____

_____

_____

_____

_____

_____

_____

_____

_____

_____

_____

_____

_____

_____

_____

_____

_____

Section B: Writing

You are advised to spend about 45 minutes on this section.

Write in full sentences.

You are reminded of the need to plan your answer.

You should leave enough time to check your work at the end.

5 You are going to enter a creative writing competition.

Your entry will be judged by a panel of people of your own age.

Either: Write a description suggested by this picture:

Or:

Write the opening part of a story that begins with a desperate chase in a bleak setting.

(24 marks for content and organisation
16 marks for technical accuracy)
[40 marks]

_____

_____

_____

_____

END OF QUESTIONS

Paper 2: Writers' viewpoints and perspectives

Time allowed: 1 hour 45 minutes

Materials

For this paper you must have:
- Source A and Source B – which are located on pages 22–4.

Instructions

- Answer all questions.
- Answer the questions in the space provided, continuing onto a separate sheet if needed.
- Do all rough work in a notebook or on separate sheets of paper.
- You must refer to the Sources provided.
- You should not use a dictionary.

Information

- The marks for questions are shown in brackets.
- The maximum mark for this paper is 80.
- There are 40 marks for Section A and 40 marks for Section B.
- You are reminded of the need for good English and clear presentation in your answers.
- The quality of your reading is assessed in Section A.
- The quality of your writing is assessed in Section B.

Advice

- You are advised to spend about 15 minutes reading through the Sources and all five questions you have to answer.
- You should make sure you leave sufficient time to check your answers.

Source A – 21st Century non-fiction

This Source is an extract from an article written for *The Guardian* by a father contemplating the long school summer holidays.

Why working parents like me dread the summer holidays

The Guardian, Friday 22 July 2016, by Andy Dawson (theguardian.com)

Before it appears that I'm some kind of villainous dad, I need to establish that ever since they came into my life, my overriding purpose in life has been to be a diligent, devoted parent to my two children [...]

5   But each year when the summer holidays loom I transform into a twitchy, cranky mess, breaking out in cold sweats and clawing at my own skin as I fret about what's to come once they've been turfed through the school gate for the last time.

If you're a working parent of a school-age child, you know exactly what I'm talking about. If you haven't been dreading the onset of the summer break and the impossible work/parenting juggle that comes with it, you're a liar.

10 On one hand I'm incredibly lucky that, as a freelance writer, I get to work from home and am usually unimpeded by obstacles such as fixed working hours or a remote workplace (although the thought of such sanctuary has its appeal).

Having said that, I also have to write 30,000 words of a book between now and the end of August, which means that it's going to get really, really tense around here when the children's 15   mum is occupied with her proper job. In fact, I had to get out of bed at 5am just to find the time to write this piece, but that's OK.

We're not short of things to do – we live a couple of miles from the north-east coast and a short car ride away from the majestic Northumberland countryside, so day trips are well catered for. Plus there's the new-found wonders of Pokémon Go – less than a week into that 20   craze and we're all sporting [...] tans from extended adventures in the sunshine.

But the book deadline means I can't afford to take a sustained period off work, which leaves us with those days when we're all rattling around the house, getting right on each other's wick.

As such, a domestic state of emergency kicks into operation. The house as we know it ceases to exist. Any kind of structure or order flies out of the window, with chores abandoned

25   and the ironing pile relocated to a hidden bubble of space behind the settee so we can all
pretend it isn't there.

Bits of Lego, random action figures and hundreds of collector cards are strewn all over the
floor, with the living room now resembling a toy shop that has been ransacked in a riot.

Try as I might to get some work done, it's as laborious as pushing a golf ball up a custard
30   mountain with the tip of my nose. The kids seem to have developed some sort of innate,
unspoken tag team system. The moment I sit down after finishing a 20-minute football match
in the garden with the boy one, the girl one appears and wants to know if she can have some
strawberries or whether I know why the printer has stopped working.

You know you're broken when you find yourself on eBay, researching the cost of those paper
35   boiler suits that decorators and lab technicians wear. We'll all look daft, but it'll cut right
down on laundry.

There's always the option of farming them out (in the nicest possible way, obviously) to
someone else, but the cost is too great, be it financially (childcare fees are exorbitant) or
emotionally (their grandparents are now shattered husks, wrecked from more than a decade
40   of ad hoc babysitting).

It's not just the days – the summer holidays blight your evenings too. Extensions to regular
bedtimes mean that the younglings are mooching about the house well after 11pm. Thinking
of catching up on the last series of Game of Thrones at the end of a hard day's life-juggling?
Better get your finger poised over the remote in case they wander in from their respective
45   leisure spaces to submit some kind of random cheese enquiry or ask if you can evict a spider
from the bathroom.

The whole thing is a lot like regular parenting, only filtered through a psychedelic
kaleidoscope and played out at three times its usual speed. You quickly realise how much
of the strain of child-rearing is carried by the education system, and you vow never to make
50   one of those snide remarks about teachers knocking off at half three each day and spending
most of their lives on holiday.

Source B – 19th Century literary non-fiction

This Source is taken from a letter written by George Gissing, an English novelist who lived from 1857–1903. His letter describes a national bank holiday in 1882.

It is Bank Holiday to-day, and the streets are overcrowded with swarms of people. Never is so clearly to be seen the vulgarity of the people as at these holiday times. Their notion of a holiday is to rush in crowds to some sweltering place, such as the Crystal Palace,[1] and there sit and drink and quarrel themselves into stupidity. Miserable children are lugged about,

5   yelling at the top of their voices, and are beaten because they yell. Troops of hideous creatures drive wildly about the town in gigs,[2] donkey-carts, cabbage-carts, dirt-carts, and think it enjoyment. The pleasure of peace and quietness, of rest for body and mind, is not understood. Thousands are tempted by cheap trips to go off for the day to the seaside, and succeed in wearying themselves to death, for the sake of eating a greasy meal in a

10   Margate Coffee-shop, and getting five minutes' glimpse of the sea through eyes blinded with dirt and perspiration. Places like Hampstead Heath and the various parks and commons are packed with screeching drunkards, one general mass of dust and heat and rage and exhaustion. Yet this is the best kind of holiday the people are capable of.

It is utterly absurd, this idea of setting aside single days for great public holidays. It will never

15   do anything but harm. What we want is a general shortening of the working hours all year round, so that, for instance, all labour would be over at 4 o'clock in the afternoon. Then the idea of hours of leisure would become familiar to the people and they would learn to make some sensible use of them. Of course this is impossible so long as we work for working's sake. All the world's work – all that is really necessary for the health and comfort and even

20   luxury of mankind – could be performed in three or four hours of each day. There is so much labour just because there is so much money-grubbing. Every man has to fight for a living with his neighbour, and the grocer who keeps his shop open till half an hour after midnight has an advantage over him who closes at twelve. Work in itself is *not an end; only a means;* but we nowadays make it an end, and three-fourths of the world cannot understand anything else.

Glossary

Crystal Palace[1] – a large, glass building in London which was often used for shows, concerts and exhibitions.
gigs[2] – a gig is a two-wheeled carriage pulled by a horse.

Section A: Reading

Answer **all** questions in this section.
You are advised to spend about 45 minutes on this section.

1 Read again the first part of **Source A, lines 1 to 16**.

Choose **four** statements below which are TRUE.

- Tick the boxes of the ones that you think are true.
- Choose a maximum of four statements.

[4 marks]

A Andy Dawson claims to be devoted to his children. ☑

B Andy Dawson dreads the end of term. ☑

C As a writer, Andy Dawson faces fewer work complications than some other parents. ☐

D Andy Dawson has never wanted to work in a remote location. ☐

E Andy Dawson believes other parents share his feelings about school holidays. ☑

F Andy Dawson is not concerned about his approaching deadline. ☐

G The children's mother also works from home. ☐

H Andy Dawson always gets up at 5am to work. ☑

2 You need to refer to **Source A** and **Source B** for this question:

Use details from **both** Sources. Write a summary of the differences between the problems that these writers associate with holidays.

[8 marks]

3 You now need to refer **only** to **Source B**, the letter by Gissing.

How does Gissing use language to suggest that bank holidays make people unhappy?

[12 marks]

4 For this question, you need to refer to the **whole of Source A** together with **Source B**.

Compare how the two writers convey their feelings about holidays.

In your answer, you could:

■ compare their different feelings
■ compare the methods they use to convey their feelings
■ support your ideas with references to both texts.

[16 marks]

_____

_____

_____

_____

_____

_____

_____

_____

_____

_____

_____

_____

_____

_____

_____

_____

_____

_____

_____

_____

_____

_____

Section B: Writing

You are advised to spend about 45 minutes on this section.
Write in full sentences.
You are reminded of the need to plan your answer.
You should leave enough time to check your work at the end.

---

5 'School summer holidays are too long. Most students get bored as the weeks drag on and they forget much of what they have learned. Students should spend more time at school.'

Write an article for a broadsheet newspaper in which you explain your point of view on this statement.

(24 marks for content and organisation
16 marks for technical accuracy)

[40 marks]

_____

_____

_____

_____

_____

_____

_____

_____

_____

_____

_____

_____

_____

_____

_____

_____

_____

_____

END OF QUESTIONS

Answers and sample responses

Paper 1: Section A

1 (AO1)

Any four or more answers from the following:
- It was loud.
- It 'pealed out from somewhere far off'.
- It became louder and more urgent.
- It was vehement.
- It was an 'agonized cry' that 'swept through the silent night'.
- A 'new sound mingled with it, a deep, muttered rumble'.
- It was 'musical and yet menacing, rising and falling like the low, constant murmur of the sea'.

2 (AO2)

Possible answers

- Exclamation marks are used to convey a sense of urgency in the line '"The hound!" cried Holmes. "Come, Watson, come! Great heavens, if we are too late!"'
- There are three of these exclamation marks so the writer is using a pattern of three to highlight the strength of Holmes's emotions.
- These same sentences are short and sharp to suggest that Holmes is in a rush and can't waste words.
- The combination of the verb 'running' with the adverb 'swiftly' suggests fast movement.
- A simile is used in 'I saw Holmes put his hand to his forehead like a man distracted'. Here 'distracted' means agitated or deeply troubled, suggesting that Holmes could not behave in a logical manner.
- Holmes says, 'Fool that I was to hold my hand. And you, Watson, see what comes of abandoning your charge!' By using the noun 'fool' he is being self-critical. He follows this up by blaming Watson for leaving Sir Henry. This comment is marked by an exclamation mark to show strong emotion.
- The complex sentence which begins with the words 'Blindly we ran through the gloom, blundering against boulders' uses alliteration since 'blindly', 'blundering' and 'boulders' all begin with 'b'. This alliteration draws attention to the men's stumbling movements and the obstacles in their path.
- The verb 'blundering' begins a cumulative list of verbs ('panting', 'rushing' and 'heading'), all suggesting ongoing action.
- This sentence is also broken up by commas which may represent Holmes's shortness of breath. This idea is reinforced by the writer's use of the verb 'panting'.

- The adverb 'blindly' suggests that Holmes was not thinking about what he was doing.
- The verb 'blundering' implies carelessness.
- The verb 'rushing' shows that he was moving very quickly.
- The words 'forcing our way through gorse bushes' imply that the route was painful because gorse bushes have thorns on them and a rational person would avoid the pain of being scratched.
- The writer's use of the adverb 'eagerly' could suggest impatience or anxiety.

Sample student responses

Level	Skills descriptors
Higher	Shows detailed and perceptive understanding of *language*: You select a very well-chosen range of details from the text. You analyse the effects of the writer's choices of *language*. You make sophisticated use of accurate terminology.
Mid	Shows clear understanding of *language*: You select a relevant range of details from the text. You clearly explain the effects of the writer's choices of *language*. You use accurate terminology.

Higher Level

The opening of this extract uses a series of short, sharp, commanding sentences punctuated by exclamation marks to convey Holmes's desperation. In the same lines, the writer employs the pattern of three to highlight the extremity of Holmes's feelings: '"The hound!" cried Holmes. "Come, Watson, come! Great heavens, if we are too late!"'

Holmes indicates desperation when he flings out accusations: 'Fool that I was to hold my hand' and 'Watson, see what comes of abandoning your charge!' By using the noun 'fool' to describe himself Holmes is being highly self-critical and he quickly follows this up by also blaming Watson. In addition, the simile 'Holmes put his hand to his forehead like a man distracted' implies that Holmes is deeply troubled and has abandoned his usual calm reasoning abilities.

The dramatic use of a complex alliterative sentence beginning 'Blindly we ran through the gloom, blundering against boulders' reflects a sense of rushing momentum where the verb 'blundering' begins a list of 'ing' verbs ('panting', 'rushing' and 'heading'), with a cumulative effect suggesting continuous ongoing action. This sentence is also broken up by commas which might represent Holmes's shortness of breath as he rushes forwards. Finally, the adverb 'eagerly' suggests Holmes's anxiety and impatience.

Mid Level

The writer says Holmes 'had started running swiftly over the moor'. The adverb 'swiftly' emphasises that Holmes is moving very fast and this speed shows his desperation. When we are told that he is 'like a man distracted' it has the effect of making us realise that Holmes felt very upset. Here the writer uses a simile which gives us a clear picture of Holmes being 'distracted' which means troubled. We can also tell that Holmes is rushing because of the alliteration used in 'Blindly we ran through the gloom, blundering against boulders, forcing our way through gorse bushes, panting up hills and rushing down slopes'. The verbs here create a lot of movement while the alliteration draws attention to his route, helping us to imagine a scene where Holmes is rushing across the moors in desperation.

3 (AO2)

Possible answers

- The text is structured so that it propels readers quickly through the action.
- The piece begins with Holmes jumping to his feet, suggesting that something dramatic is happening.
- The reader is immediately drawn into the urgency of the situation by sharp snatches of dialogue.
- This dialogue is intermingled with descriptions of the noise in order to draw the reader's attention back to the strange sound and make them want to find out what it is.
- Around the middle of the extract, the focus shifts when Holmes starts running, with Watson following quickly behind him.
- The reader is rushed along, accompanying the two men as they dash 'blindly' across the moors.
- Like the men, the text itself is heading towards the place where the strange sound seems to be coming from.
- The noise is presented as getting closer and closer until it is located on the men's left.
- As Holmes and Watson approach the cliff, the focus of the text gradually narrows towards the body.
- Conan Doyle brings his readers increasingly closer to this dead body, which changes from a 'vague outline' to a 'definite shape'. Then the writer focuses in even more to reveal 'the body of Sir Henry Baskerville'.
- Further closely observed details about the body are provided when the reader is told that it is dressed in a distinctive 'tweed suit'.

- At the end of this episode the writer moves his focus away from the body and back to Holmes's and Watson's horrified reactions to it.

Sample student responses

Level	Skills descriptors
Higher	Shows detailed and perceptive understanding of *structural* features: You select a very well-chosen range of examples. You analyse the effects of these features. You refer to them by making sophisticated use of accurate terminology.
Mid	Shows clear understanding of *structural* features: You select a range of relevant examples. You refer to them by making clear use of accurate terminology.

Higher Level

The text, which is about a desperate rush to prevent murder, is structured so that the reader feels he/she is being propelled quickly through it: from the opening when Holmes jumps to his feet, to the men's chase across the moors and then finally to the dreadful moment when the body is discovered and identified. Readers are immediately drawn into the urgency of the situation by snatches of dialogue such as 'No, there!' and by descriptions of a strange cry.

Around the middle of the extract, the focus shifts to the chase as Holmes starts 'running swiftly' over the moor with Watson 'at his heels'. The reader is then rushed along, accompanying these men through a bleak terrain of 'boulders' and 'gorse bushes'. Like them, the text is 'heading always in the direction whence those dreadful sounds had come'. However, as they approach the cliff, the writer's focus narrows dramatically as it moves closer and closer to the dead body, which is conveyed first as a 'vague outline' and then as a 'definite shape' and finally as 'the body of Sir Henry Baskerville' dressed in his distinctive 'tweed suit'. Finally, the writer shifts attention away from the victim and back to Holmes and Watson as their horrified reactions to their discovery are revealed.

Mid Level

The writer focuses the reader's attention on Holmes jumping up at the beginning of this episode. This shows us that this text is about something dramatic. Then he reveals what has caught Holmes's attention by describing the noise when he writes 'The cry had been loud'. This involves readers in the action because they wonder what the sound is.

The writer then shifts the focus away from the noise, describing the two men running towards it. Holmes runs with Watson 'at his heels'. This running section continues at a rapid pace as the writer draws attention to the men 'forcing our way through gorse bushes, panting up hills and rushing down slopes'. Throughout this part the reader feels like he or she is with the men on their chase.

Next the body is revealed at a distance. At first it seems unclear but gradually the writer moves his focus closer and closer until it is identified. Holmes and Watson become distressed when they realise the dead man is Sir Henry so the writer changes focus by shifting attention to their emotions rather than the dead body.

4 (AO4)

Possible answers

- The question 'But, hark, what is that?' makes us want to read on to discover what has been heard.
- A 'low moan' sounds as if somebody is suffering or in pain.
- The words 'There it was again upon our left!' give us the impression that the men are moving continually closer to the sound. The exclamation mark suggests desperation and urgency.
- The description of the cliff face as 'sheer' and 'jagged' implies that the setting was sinister and dangerous.
- The men 'ran' towards the sound, which suggests they were in a desperate hurry.
- The writer builds tension by revealing the body slowly. Conan Doyle encourages readers to imagine a 'vague outline' changing to become a 'definite shape'.
- The way that the writer has positioned the body 'face downward' delays its identification and builds the tension further.
- The line 'Not a whisper, not a rustle, rose now from the dark figure over which we stooped' suggests a tense pause in the action which contrasts with the earlier rush.
- The descriptions of the body ('horrible angle', 'crushed skull' and 'body hunched') are extremely vivid and effective at painting a clear, if brutal, picture.
- The fact that the body can only be seen by the 'gleam of' a match suggests that each part is revealed faintly through flickering light.

- They had to light a match because it was dark, which makes the scene seem more eerie.
- Night-time seems to be a fitting setting for a murder and Gothic fiction often included sinister events set against a backdrop of darkness.
- Once the body is identified as Sir Henry Baskerville, we realise that Holmes and Watson know him. This makes the death seem more shocking.
- When the match goes out it effectively symbolises the death of hope.
- The men seem to have failed in their mission so the chase was for nothing. Now they can only experience horror and despair.
- The word 'groaned' conveys Holmes's despair and indicates (like the earlier moan) how sound is being used to enhance the drama of the piece.
- The statement 'The brute! the brute!' implies that the murderer was particularly cruel.

Sample student responses

Level	Skills descriptors
Higher	Shows perceptive and detailed evaluation: You select a very well-chosen range of details from the text. You provide a detailed critical evaluation of the effect(s) on the reader. You show perceptive understanding of the writer's methods. You develop a convincing and critical response to the statement in the question.
Mid	Shows clear and relevant evaluation: You select a relevant range of details from the text. You clearly evaluate the effect(s) on the reader. You show a clear understanding of the writer's methods. You make a clear and relevant response to the statement in the question.

Higher Level

I do agree that this episode is both tense and dramatic since it portrays the discovery of a disfigured body and the gradual and dreadful revelation of its identity. This drama begins when Holmes asks, 'hark, what is that?' Conan Doyle then goes on to define the noise as a 'low moan' (a sound normally associated with pain or suffering), creating the impression that Holmes and Watson are closing in on something sinister. From this moment, the reader shares the men's feelings of dread and anticipation as they rush towards the place where the moan emanated from. The writer's choice of setting, a 'sheer cliff' with a 'jagged face', enhances the drama because a 'sheer cliff' seems perilous and 'jagged' implies something sharp.

Conan Doyle also builds dramatic tension by slowly revealing a 'dark irregular object'. He then further delays the moment of revelation as 'the vague outline hardened into a definite shape', implying that the two men are moving closer and closer to the corpse.

The strange positioning of the body develops the tension further by obscuring its identity for even longer because it is 'prostrate' and 'face downward upon the ground'. Conan Doyle deliberately arranges the victim with 'the head doubled under him at a horrible angle', leaving his readers waiting to discover who it is.

Time seems to stand still when the narrator states, 'Not a whisper, not a rustle, rose now from the dark figure over which we stooped'. This moment of drama cleverly contrasts the previous chase with stillness and silence. Furthermore, the vivid references to a 'ghastly pool' and 'crushed skull' paint a powerful picture, implying that the victim's death was inflicted brutally and increasing the horror of the situation.

In my view, the most dramatic moment in this extract is when Holmes and Watson finally identify the body and recognise the distinctive 'tweed suit' of Sir Henry Baskerville. It is implied that they knew Sir Henry from a previous episode at 'Baker Street'. Therefore, it seems likely that they feel shocked and traumatised.

When 'the match flickered and went out' the reader realises that all hope is lost. Once this happens, I believe that the urgency and drama dissipate since all Holmes's and Watson's frantic efforts have, tragically, proved futile.

Mid Level

I agree that this passage is full of tension and drama. In fact, the subject matter is dramatic since the writer is describing two men approaching a dead body and hearing strange sounds in the middle of the night.

Holmes and Watson hear a 'low moan' which intrigues the reader and builds up tension as we seek to discover the cause of such a dreadful noise. Then, when the men approach the body, the writer reveals its identity slowly so that a 'vague outline' gradually turns out to be a person the men actually know, Sir Henry Baskerville. To add to the drama, the writer describes the body as being 'horrific' and 'grotesque', which conveys the image of something terrible. Readers also learn that the corpse has a cracked skull, which implies that a very cruel crime has been committed.

When a match goes out and the two men are left in darkness we are told that 'the hope had gone'. This breaks the tension that was created during the chase and the discovery of the body because there is nothing more that Holmes and Watson can do to help the victim. However, readers are reminded of the dramatic events that have taken place when the two men express their feelings and the murderer is called a 'brute' twice, which makes him sound very unpleasant.

Turn over for Question 5 answers

Paper 1: Section B

5 (AO5) (AO6)

Level	Skills descriptors
Higher	**Content (AO5)** Your writing is confidently matched to the purpose of the task. Your register is convincing and compelling to the audience. You use an extensive and ambitious vocabulary. Your work is well crafted. You make excellent use of linguistic devices. **Organisation (AO5)** Your writing is compelling. You make varied and inventive use of structural features. You include a range of convincing and complex ideas. Your paragraphs are linked fluently. **Technical Accuracy (AO6)** Your sentences are well defined and consistently accurate. You use a range of punctuation with a high level of accuracy. You use a full range of appropriate sentence forms for effect. You use Standard English consistently and appropriately. Your grammar is excellent. Your spelling is highly accurate, including the spelling of ambitious vocabulary.
Mid	**Content (AO5)** Your writing is generally well matched to the purpose of the task. Your register is generally matched to the audience. Your vocabulary is chosen for effect and you make some sophisticated word choices. You use linguistic devices successfully. **Organisation (AO5)** Your writing is engaging. You make effective use of structural features. You use a range of clear, connected ideas. Your paragraphs are well linked. **Technical Accuracy (AO6)** Your sentences are securely defined and mostly accurate. You use a range of punctuation, mostly with success. You use a variety of sentence forms for effect. You use Standard English appropriately. Your grammar is good. Your spelling is generally accurate, including the spelling of complex and irregular words.

Lower	**Content (AO5)** Your writing is sometimes matched to the purpose of the task. You try to match your register (level of formality) to the audience. You make an attempt to vary your vocabulary. You make some use of linguistic devices. **Organisation (AO5)** Some of your writing is clear. You use some structural features. You include a variety of linked and relevant ideas. You use paragraphs and make some use of discourse markers. **Technical Accuracy (AO6)** Most of your sentences are correctly defined. You show some control of a range of punctuation. You try to use a variety of sentence forms. You mostly use Standard English. Some of your grammar is correct. Your work includes some accurate spelling of more complex words.

Write a description suggested by the picture on page 17.

Sample student responses
Higher Level

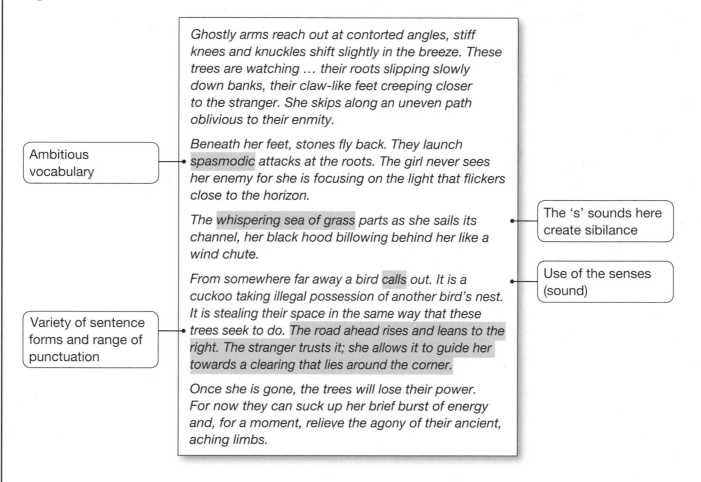

Ambitious vocabulary

Variety of sentence forms and range of punctuation

The 's' sounds here create sibilance

Use of the senses (sound)

Ghostly arms reach out at contorted angles, stiff knees and knuckles shift slightly in the breeze. These trees are watching … their roots slipping slowly down banks, their claw-like feet creeping closer to the stranger. She skips along an uneven path oblivious to their enmity.

Beneath her feet, stones fly back. They launch spasmodic attacks at the roots. The girl never sees her enemy for she is focusing on the light that flickers close to the horizon.

The whispering sea of grass parts as she sails its channel, her black hood billowing behind her like a wind chute.

From somewhere far away a bird calls out. It is a cuckoo taking illegal possession of another bird's nest. It is stealing their space in the same way that these trees seek to do. The road ahead rises and leans to the right. The stranger trusts it; she allows it to guide her towards a clearing that lies around the corner.

Once she is gone, the trees will lose their power. For now they can suck up her brief burst of energy and, for a moment, relieve the agony of their ancient, aching limbs.

Mid Level

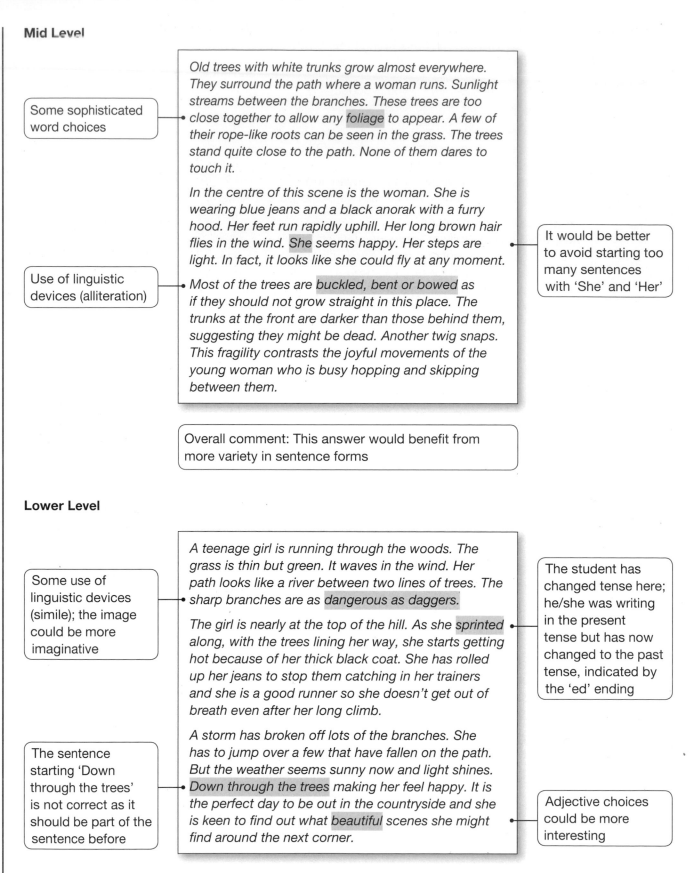

Some sophisticated word choices

Old trees with white trunks grow almost everywhere. They surround the path where a woman runs. Sunlight streams between the branches. These trees are too close together to allow any foliage to appear. A few of their rope-like roots can be seen in the grass. The trees stand quite close to the path. None of them dares to touch it.

In the centre of this scene is the woman. She is wearing blue jeans and a black anorak with a furry hood. Her feet run rapidly uphill. Her long brown hair flies in the wind. She seems happy. Her steps are light. In fact, it looks like she could fly at any moment.

It would be better to avoid starting too many sentences with 'She' and 'Her'

Use of linguistic devices (alliteration)

Most of the trees are buckled, bent or bowed as if they should not grow straight in this place. The trunks at the front are darker than those behind them, suggesting they might be dead. Another twig snaps. This fragility contrasts the joyful movements of the young woman who is busy hopping and skipping between them.

Overall comment: This answer would benefit from more variety in sentence forms

Lower Level

Some use of linguistic devices (simile); the image could be more imaginative

A teenage girl is running through the woods. The grass is thin but green. It waves in the wind. Her path looks like a river between two lines of trees. The sharp branches are as dangerous as daggers.

The girl is nearly at the top of the hill. As she sprinted along, with the trees lining her way, she starts getting hot because of her thick black coat. She has rolled up her jeans to stop them catching in her trainers and she is a good runner so she doesn't get out of breath even after her long climb.

The student has changed tense here; he/she was writing in the present tense but has now changed to the past tense, indicated by the 'ed' ending

The sentence starting 'Down through the trees' is not correct as it should be part of the sentence before

A storm has broken off lots of the branches. She has to jump over a few that have fallen on the path. But the weather seems sunny now and light shines. Down through the trees making her feel happy. It is the perfect day to be out in the countryside and she is keen to find out what beautiful scenes she might find around the next corner.

Adjective choices could be more interesting

Write the opening part of a story that begins with a desperate chase in a bleak setting.

Sample student responses

Higher Level

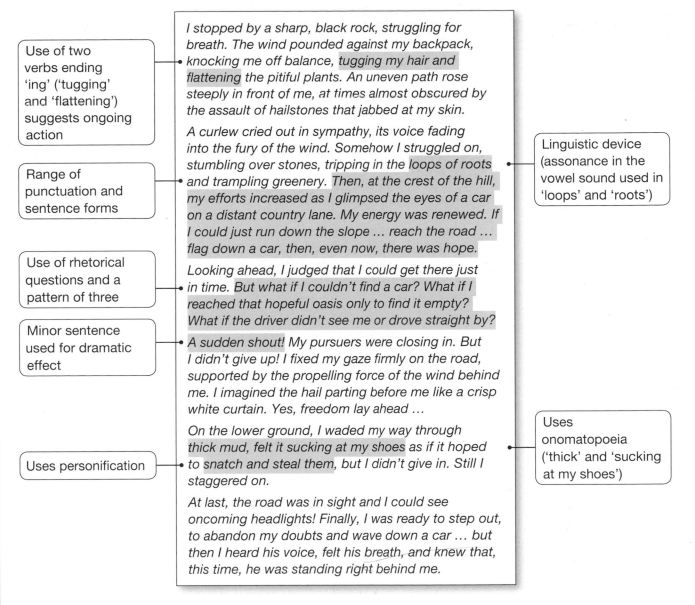

Use of two verbs ending 'ing' ('tugging' and 'flattening') suggests ongoing action

Range of punctuation and sentence forms

Use of rhetorical questions and a pattern of three

Minor sentence used for dramatic effect

Uses personification

Linguistic device (assonance in the vowel sound used in 'loops' and 'roots')

Uses onomatopoeia ('thick' and 'sucking at my shoes')

I stopped by a sharp, black rock, struggling for breath. The wind pounded against my backpack, knocking me off balance, tugging my hair and flattening the pitiful plants. An uneven path rose steeply in front of me, at times almost obscured by the assault of hailstones that jabbed at my skin.

A curlew cried out in sympathy, its voice fading into the fury of the wind. Somehow I struggled on, stumbling over stones, tripping in the loops of roots and trampling greenery. Then, at the crest of the hill, my efforts increased as I glimpsed the eyes of a car on a distant country lane. My energy was renewed. If I could just run down the slope … reach the road … flag down a car, then, even now, there was hope.

Looking ahead, I judged that I could get there just in time. But what if I couldn't find a car? What if I reached that hopeful oasis only to find it empty? What if the driver didn't see me or drove straight by?

A sudden shout! My pursuers were closing in. But I didn't give up! I fixed my gaze firmly on the road, supported by the propelling force of the wind behind me. I imagined the hail parting before me like a crisp white curtain. Yes, freedom lay ahead …

On the lower ground, I waded my way through thick mud, felt it sucking at my shoes as if it hoped to snatch and steal them, but I didn't give in. Still I staggered on.

At last, the road was in sight and I could see oncoming headlights! Finally, I was ready to step out, to abandon my doubts and wave down a car … but then I heard his voice, felt his breath, and knew that, this time, he was standing right behind me.

Mid Level

Uses 'She' too often to begin sentences; aim for more variety

> Catherine had always been faster than her sister. Her confidence grew as the gap between them increased. She gloated about her superior powers. She might rest for a while beside this silver stream so her sister could catch up.

Uses the senses (touch)

> Triumphantly, she lay back on the smooth grass under a red sky. Then she dangled her fingers idly in the icy water. She gazed up into the heavy clouds that threatened to shower her with rain, but she didn't mind for she felt hot from running. Her sister had really annoyed her and Catherine was determined to lead her hunter on a merry dance across the moor.

Slightly informal/ simplistic phrasing

> Shaking the water from her fingers, Catherine jumped up and started to sprint again, her eyes fixed on the red horizon. From time to time, she glanced backwards to observe the running figure of her sister. She knew that she was still attempting to catch her. The approach of nightfall might bring an end to their chase but for now she felt angry enough to risk anything.

'Then' was used in the previous sentence; it would be better to change this sentence opening

Uses some sophisticated vocabulary

> The blood red sky matched her volatile mood as a raindrop fell, and then another and another. Then the clouds exploded with many raindrops which quickly soaked her long blonde hair and trickled down her cheeks, but she didn't care! She confronted the rain with rage. She couldn't be bothered to look back. She was sure that her sister was losing ground and she hoped she could melt into the crimson pool of sunset.

Strong final image

Lower Level

Includes some visual details but could add further descriptive details

> Tom could see the robber sprinting across the moor. The man wore a black coat and a thick peaked cap. It seemed as if the criminal had hurt himself. He was sort of limping and struggling to carry the bag of stolen stuff he had got over his shoulder.

The word 'goods' would be a better word choice than 'stuff'

Informal phrasing

> Tom was a lot younger than this man and he was fitter too. His new spiked trainers allowed him to move easily across the uneven landscape. He set off again, following the path the man had made. He found his way by checking where the grass had been flattened. It was a muggy night and sweet dripped down his forehead.

Needs to start more sentences in ways other than 'He'

This is a spelling slip as the student has used the word 'sweet' instead of 'sweat'

> Tom was confident he would capture the criminal soon. He shouted 'Stop!' and his voice rang through the air. The robber turned back, just for a second, but then ran on. As they crossed a valley, the man stumbles again and Tom moves closer. He feels like a lion closing in on his prey.

Attempts to use a simile but it is a rather clichéd one

The tense is wrong here; the student has changed from the past ('ed' endings) to the present ('s' endings)

> The robber lurched forwards but this time his foot hit a stone and he tumbled to the ground. Tom raced up to the man and the man started cursing. At last Tom had trapped his prey but how on earth was he going to get him back?

Ending with a question makes readers want to know what will happen next in the story

Paper 2: Section A

1 (AO1)

A Andy Dawson claims to be devoted to his children. (T)

B Andy Dawson dreads the end of term. (T)

C As a writer, Andy Dawson faces fewer work complications than some other parents. (T)

D Andy Dawson has never wanted to work in a remote location. (F)

E Andy Dawson believes other parents share his feelings about school holidays. (T)

F Andy Dawson is not concerned about his approaching deadline. (F)

G The children's mother also works from home. (F)

H Andy Dawson always gets up at 5am to work. (F)

2 (AO1)

Possible answers

Problems associated with holidays in Source A by Andy Dawson

- It is 'impossible' to juggle work and parenting responsibilities.
- He has to get up early at 5am in order to keep to deadlines.
- The children need entertaining but he can't 'afford to' take time off work.
- The family begin to irritate each other as they get on 'each other's wick'.
- The house gets very untidy and laundry builds up into a 'domestic state of emergency'.
- He can't get on with his work due to interruptions. These make doing work feel 'as laborious as pushing a golf ball up a custard mountain'.
- The children stay up late and 'blight' Dawson's evenings.

Problems associated with holidays in Source B by George Gissing

- People don't know how to make 'sensible use' of their days off.
- People become 'weary' in their search for the sea and cheap food.
- There is lots of 'dust' and 'dirt'.
- People are more used to working 'for work's sake' than enjoying their leisure time.
- On holiday days people 'drive wildly about the town'.
- The streets get 'overcrowded with swarms of people'.
- People get noisy, and become 'screeching drunkards'.
- The children become 'miserable' when they are 'lugged about'.

Sample student responses

Level	Skills descriptors
Higher	Shows perceptive synthesis and interpretation of both texts: You select well-chosen details from the texts. These details are relevant to the focus of the question. You make perceptive inferences from both texts. Your statements show perceptive differences between texts.
Mid	Shows clear synthesis and interpretation of both texts: You select clear details from the texts. These details are relevant to the focus of the question. You make clear inferences from both texts. Your statements show clear differences between texts.

Higher Level

Both Andy Dawson and George Gissing think that holidays cause difficulties and they both discuss these problems in relation to work. Dawson shows no real inclination to enjoy the holidays with his children and the majority of his problems arise because of what he calls the 'impossible work/parenting juggle'. He is reduced to getting up at 5am to meet work deadlines because his children demand constant entertainment and attention.

Gissing, on the other hand, feels that the general public would like to enjoy bank holidays but they don't know how because they spend most of their time working 'for work's sake'. Furthermore, holiday chaos features in both texts: in the Dawson article there is internal chaos as the house is thrown into a 'domestic state of emergency' as laundry builds up, while Gissing describes external chaos consisting of overcrowded streets, parks full of 'screeching drunkards' and people driving about 'wildly'.

In both texts it is suggested that children cause problems during holidays. Dawson and his children find it impossible to co-exist peacefully and end up 'getting right on each other's wick'. Likewise, in the Gissing extract, miserable children cry after being 'lugged' around the town. Then they are 'beaten because they yell' which causes more misery.

Mid Level

Both writers suggest that holidays cause problems. Andy Dawson's main problem is that he has to look after his children, which means that he can't get on with his work. The children annoy him by staying up too late, asking him to play football and fix the printer. He seems to have a rather negative attitude towards his children. On the other hand, Gissing has a negative attitude towards the crowds of ordinary people who spend their bank holidays having fun outside. He claims that these people work so much that they have no idea how to enjoy a proper holiday.

Dawson's main problem is that he is always thinking about work and not about having fun with his children. He believes that trying to get on with his work is as 'laborious as pushing a golf ball up a custard mountain', which would be almost impossible. In contrast, Gissing focuses on how people behave badly on bank holidays and claims that they get loud and drunk.

3 (AO2)

Possible answers

- Gissing states that the streets are 'overcrowded' and that the people 'rush in crowds'. The noun 'crowds' suggests that holidaymakers may be following others rather than doing what they want.
- The verb 'rush' implies haste which is not something associated with peace or relaxation.
- The people are described rushing to 'some sweltering place'. The adjective 'sweltering' implies somewhere unbearably hot, which would be uncomfortable.
- Gissing explains that people 'sit and drink and quarrel themselves into stupidity'. His repetition of the conjunction 'and' implies a connected sequence of events. People who are quarrelling are not happy.
- The noun 'stupidity' implies that people drink themselves senseless and this could prevent them from enjoying their holiday.
- The children are clearly unhappy as they are described using the adjective 'miserable'. We are also told that children are 'lugged' about. The verb 'to lug' means to carry with difficulty and this implies the children are viewed as a burden.
- These children are 'yelling at the top of their voices, and are beaten because they yell'. Their distress is punished by their parents who are presumably unhappy about the noise.
- Those who go to the seaside 'succeed in wearying themselves to death'. The phrase 'to death' is often used to convey negative emotions.
- The adjective 'greasy' is used to describe a 'meal in a Margate Coffee-shop'. Greasy food is oily and it would not be enjoyable to eat.
- When people try to look at the sea, they find their eyes are 'blinded with dirt and perspiration'. The nouns 'dirt' and 'perspiration' are both negative and make readers think that the people are physically uncomfortable.

- This idea of dirt is supported by another sentence employing the conjunction 'and': 'one general mass of dust and heat and rage and exhaustion'. Here the 'ands' extend the sentence to suggest that the people's suffering was long-term. This sentence also reminds us that the people were hot, quarrelling, tired and dirty.

Sample student responses

Level	Skills descriptors
Higher	Shows detailed and perceptive understanding of *language*:
	You select a range of well-chosen details from the text.
	You analyse the effects of the writer's choices of *language*.
	You make sophisticated and accurate use of terminology.
Mid	Shows clear understanding of *language*:
	You select a range of relevant details from the text.
	You clearly explain the effects of the writer's choices of *language*.
	You make clear and accurate use of terminology.

Higher Level

Throughout this extract Gissing uses language associated with heat, dirt, anger and overcrowding to suggest that holidays make people unhappy. Holidaymakers are described as rushing 'in crowds' to 'sweltering' places. The adjective 'sweltering' gives us an impression of uncomfortable heat while the noun 'crowds' suggests that nobody has room to move. He develops this initial picture of suffering by using the adjective 'miserable' to describe the children who are 'lugged' about by their parents and beaten when they 'yell'. The verb 'lugged' implies that parents view their children as burdens and we could infer that they were probably smacked because their crying was an irritation to the adults.

Gissing makes a trip to the seaside sound very unappealing as he lists a number of possible causes of unhappiness. A café meal is described using the adjective 'greasy' which makes it sound oily and unappetising. The people weary themselves 'to death' and this phrase has very negative connotations. Eyes are blinded with 'dirt and perspiration', two nouns that develop the impression of heat and dirtiness.

Gissing twice uses the conjunction 'and' to extend sentences which describe people's unhappiness. Initially he states that people 'sit and drink and quarrel themselves into stupidity'. In this instance, his use of 'and' suggests a process of unfortunate but interconnected events. Quarrelling is not something that we normally associate with happiness and being drunk would also prevent any real enjoyment of the holiday. Near the end of his first paragraph, Gissing uses the word 'and' in a similar way when he describes people as 'one general mass of dust and heat and rage and exhaustion'. Here the conjunction is used to draw the reader's attention to each of the problems the holidaymakers face. This sentence also supports many of Gissing's earlier points since 'dust' reminds us of 'dirt', 'heat' reminds us of 'sweltering' and 'perspiration', 'rage' reminds us that the people are quarrelling and 'exhaustion' can be linked to the idea of people wearying themselves 'to death'.

Mid Level

The writer describes the unpleasant conditions that people have to endure on bank holidays. They go to 'sweltering' places and 'rush' about in 'crowds'. This would make anybody feel unhappy as rushing about in the heat is not pleasant.

The children are described using the adjective 'miserable' and their parents smack them when they cry. They are 'lugged about, yelling at the top of their voices', which shows us that they were very unhappy. The verb 'lugged' suggests they are being dragged about, which seems like their parents don't care about their feelings much.

Gissing also uses very negative language to describe a trip to the seaside where the food is 'greasy' and the people's eyes get 'blinded with dirt and perspiration' which means that they can't see the sea because they are hot and sweaty. This would not be what they expected when they set off for a day trip and it would probably make them unhappy.

The writer also tells us that the parks and commons are full of 'screeching drunkards' and 'screeching' sounds noisy and unpleasant. There is also a long sentence describing a mass of 'dust and heat and rage and exhaustion' which sounds like nobody is happy because they are hot, grumpy and tired.

4 (AO3)

Possible answers

- Both writers seem to have predominantly negative feelings about holidays.
- Dawson feels that there is no time for work during the holidays, which become an 'impossible work/parenting juggle'.
- Gissing suggests there is no time for leisure in working life so people don't know how to relax when they are on holiday.
- The two men adopt very different tones.
- Dawson's tone is humorous and his feelings are conveyed in an amusing way, often through deliberate over-exaggeration such as 'breaking out in cold sweats'.
- He addresses the reader directly, using the word 'you' in order to encourage us to empathise with his feelings, and he shares amusing domestic anecdotes.
- Gissing writes from a more distant, judgemental position, remaining detached from the scenes he describes.
- Gissing feels that holidays make children 'miserable' and then their parents beat them 'because they yell'.
- Dawson feels that his children deliberately make him suffer as they have invented 'some sort of unspoken tag system' to make sure that he is constantly interrupted.
- The structure of each text reveals the writer's feelings.
- Gissing opens his letter with an immediate description of streets crowded 'with swarms of people'. The collective noun 'swarms' is usually used to describe flies or bees.
- He uses another animalistic term when he refers to holidaymakers as 'hideous creatures'.
- In his article, Dawson implies that the holidays soon have him 'clawing at [his] own skin'. The term 'clawing' is also associated with animals.
- In his second paragraph, Gissing changes to a more reflective tone as he tries to suggest that work is the cause of holiday problems.
- Dawson also becomes reflective when he thinks about 'how much of the strain of child-rearing is carried by the education system'.

Sample student responses

Level	Skills descriptors
Higher	Compares ideas and perspectives in a perceptive way: You analyse how writers' methods are used. You select a range of well-chosen supporting detail from both texts. You show a detailed understanding of the different ideas and perspectives in both texts.
Mid	Compares ideas and perspectives in a clear and relevant way: You explain clearly how writers' methods are used. You select relevant detail from both texts. You show a clear understanding of the different ideas and perspectives in both texts.

Higher Level

Both Andy Dawson and George Gissing have negative feelings about holidays but while Dawson suggests that it is the holidays that stop him being able to work, because of the 'impossible work/parenting juggle', Gissing implies that it is work that stops people enjoying their holidays since most of them 'work for work's sake' and don't know how to relax.

Dawson adopts a humorous, conversational, tone. He shares amusing anecdotes from his life and addresses the reader as 'you' to encourage empathy. Gissing writes from a more detached position which could infer that he feels superior to most holidaymakers because he dislikes crowded noisy places and prefers 'the pleasure of peace and quietness'. His use of alliteration emphasises the value of such tranquillity. Dawson also dreams of relaxing during summer evenings but he feels that holidays 'blight' this precious free time because of 'extensions to regular bedtimes'. The word 'blight' implies that his free time is spoilt and disrupted.

Disruption is indeed a key theme for both writers. Gissing criticises those who disturb the peace by driving 'wildly about the town in gigs, donkey-carts, cabbage-carts, dirt-carts'. It is noticeable that these carts all have negative implications, as if they are unsuitable for people. His reference to 'dirt-carts' also supports his ongoing suggestion that holidays cause mess, filth and 'dust'. Similarly, Dawson acknowledges that holidays can become chaotic when he loses control of the chores and the living room resembles 'a toy shop that has been ransacked in a riot'.

Both writers use derogatory language to reveal their feelings about others. Gissing refers to drunken holidaymakers 'screeching', a sound normally associated with birds, while Dawson claims that his children are 'mooching' about, implying that they may be bored or listless. He is clearly irritated when he suggests that his children have developed 'some sort of innate, unspoken tag team system' in order to make sure that he is constantly pestered. Gissing also implies that children annoy their parents since they beat them 'because they yell'.

The benefits of holiday outings and excursions are discussed in both texts but here the writers' feelings clearly differ. Dawson feels that there are 'majestic' places to visit, but Gissing paints a grim picture of a visit to the seaside where visitors can only glimpse the sea through 'eyes blinded with dirt and perspiration'.

The structure of these texts is designed to reveal more about the writers' feelings. Gissing begins his piece with an immediate description of bank holiday chaos where 'streets are overcrowded with swarms of people'. Interestingly, we would normally use the collective noun 'swarms' to describe flies or wasps. He is implying that holidays dehumanise people, and this can also be seen when he calls the holidaymakers 'hideous creatures'. Similarly, Dawson feels that holidays cause negative transformations. He suggests that school holidays reduce him to a point where he is 'clawing at [his] own skin'. This description is clearly an example of humorous exaggeration but, like 'swarms', 'clawing' is a term normally associated with animals.

Once Gissing has given vent to his critical feelings, he becomes more reflective in the second half of his letter. He tries to explain why holidays are so problematic by suggesting that people spend too much time working. Dawson also becomes reflective when he realises 'how much of the strain of child-rearing is carried by the education system'.

Mid Level

Dawson reveals his feelings about holidays in a humorous way by encouraging us to imagine incidents from his own life. He involves readers directly in the action by using the word 'you' throughout his article. He feels that holidays interrupt his work, but as he has a deadline to meet, he gets very irritated by his children, although he tries not to show this as he wants to be a good father.

Gissing draws attention to the way that people behave on holidays and he seems to feel that their behaviour is totally inappropriate. He appears to judge others and to view them from a very critical viewpoint. He calls them 'hideous creatures', which suggests that he feels they are behaving like animals, and he clearly disapproves of their drunken 'screeching'.

Both writers suggest that children cause irritation during holidays. Dawson is annoyed because his children keep deliberately interrupting him, while Gissing observes children being 'lugged' about and then yelling, which makes their parents smack them.

After spending a whole paragraph expressing his critical views about holidaymakers, Gissing attempts to explain why people can't enjoy their leisure. He feels that it would be better to give them shorter

working days rather than bank holidays because then they might learn how to enjoy themselves. Dawson devotes most of his article to explaining why he feels so frustrated but he does so in an amusing way by sharing a number of anecdotes to illustrate his feelings. For example, the girl interrupts him because she 'wants to know if she can have some strawberries'. I think this is funny because it seems very realistic.

Turn over for Question 5 answers

PART TWO: YORK NOTES PRACTICE TEST ONE

Paper 2: Section B

5 (AO5) (AO6)

Level	Skills descriptors
Higher	**Content (AO5)** Your writing is confidently matched to the purpose of the task. Your register is convincing and compelling to the audience. You use an extensive and ambitious vocabulary. Your work is well crafted. You make excellent use of linguistic devices. **Organisation (AO5)** Your writing is compelling. You make varied and inventive use of structural features. You include a range of convincing and complex ideas. Your paragraphs are linked fluently. **Technical Accuracy (AO6)** Your sentences are well defined and consistently accurate. You use a range of punctuation with a high level of accuracy. You use a full range of appropriate sentence forms for effect. You use Standard English consistently and appropriately. Your grammar is excellent. Your spelling is highly accurate, including the spelling of ambitious vocabulary.
Mid	**Content (AO5)** Your writing is generally well matched to the purpose of the task. Your register is generally matched to the audience. Your vocabulary is chosen for effect and you make some sophisticated word choices. You use linguistic devices successfully. **Organisation (AO5)** Your writing is engaging. You make effective use of structural features. You use a range of clear, connected ideas. Your paragraphs are well linked. **Technical Accuracy (AO6)** Your sentences are securely defined and mostly accurate. You use a range of punctuation, mostly with success. You use a variety of sentence forms for effect. You use Standard English appropriately. Your grammar is good. Your spelling is generally accurate, including the spelling of complex and irregular words.
Lower	**Content** (AO5) Your writing is sometimes matched to the purpose of the task. You try to match your register (level of formality) to the audience. You make an attempt to vary your vocabulary. You make some use of linguistic devices. **Organisation (AO5)** Some of your writing is clear. You use some structural features. You include a variety of linked and relevant ideas. You use paragraphs and make some use of discourse markers.

48

Lower (continued)	**Technical Accuracy (AO6)** Most of your sentences are correctly defined. You show some control of a range of punctuation. You try to use a variety of sentence forms. You mostly use Standard English. Some of your grammar is correct. Your work includes some accurate spelling of more complex words.

6 (AO5) (AO6)

Sample student responses
Higher Level

This opening engages the reader because the scene is depicted so clearly

Use of literary device (alliteration)

Direct address draws in the reader

Addresses the reader directly

Humorous personal tone

Uses repetition to reiterate a key point

Use of anecdote

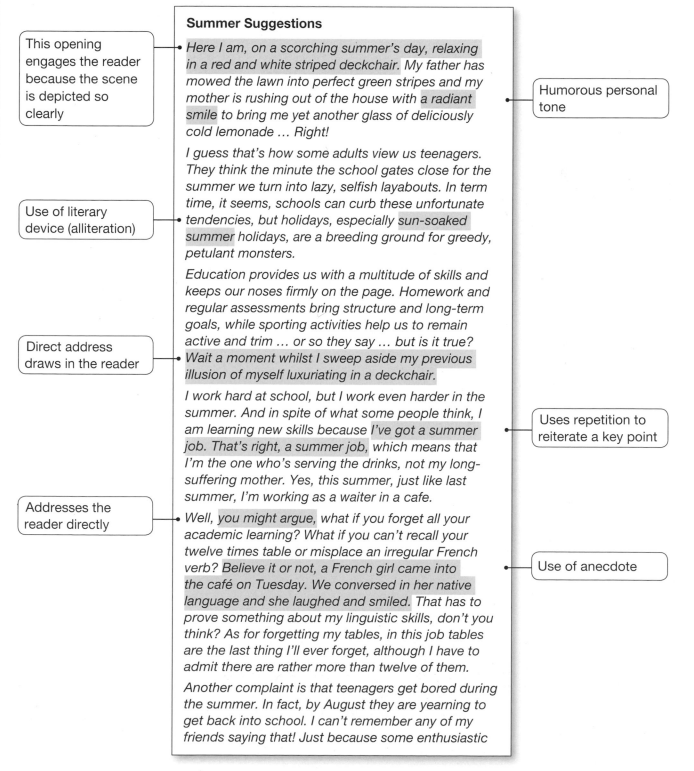

Summer Suggestions

Here I am, on a scorching summer's day, relaxing in a red and white striped deckchair. My father has mowed the lawn into perfect green stripes and my mother is rushing out of the house with a radiant smile to bring me yet another glass of deliciously cold lemonade … Right!

I guess that's how some adults view us teenagers. They think the minute the school gates close for the summer we turn into lazy, selfish layabouts. In term time, it seems, schools can curb these unfortunate tendencies, but holidays, especially sun-soaked summer holidays, are a breeding ground for greedy, petulant monsters.

Education provides us with a multitude of skills and keeps our noses firmly on the page. Homework and regular assessments bring structure and long-term goals, while sporting activities help us to remain active and trim … or so they say … but is it true? Wait a moment whilst I sweep aside my previous illusion of myself luxuriating in a deckchair.

I work hard at school, but I work even harder in the summer. And in spite of what some people think, I am learning new skills because I've got a summer job. That's right, a summer job, which means that I'm the one who's serving the drinks, not my long-suffering mother. Yes, this summer, just like last summer, I'm working as a waiter in a cafe.

Well, you might argue, what if you forget all your academic learning? What if you can't recall your twelve times table or misplace an irregular French verb? Believe it or not, a French girl came into the café on Tuesday. We conversed in her native language and she laughed and smiled. That has to prove something about my linguistic skills, don't you think? As for forgetting my tables, in this job tables are the last thing I'll ever forget, although I have to admit there are rather more than twelve of them.

Another complaint is that teenagers get bored during the summer. In fact, by August they are yearning to get back into school. I can't remember any of my friends saying that! Just because some enthusiastic

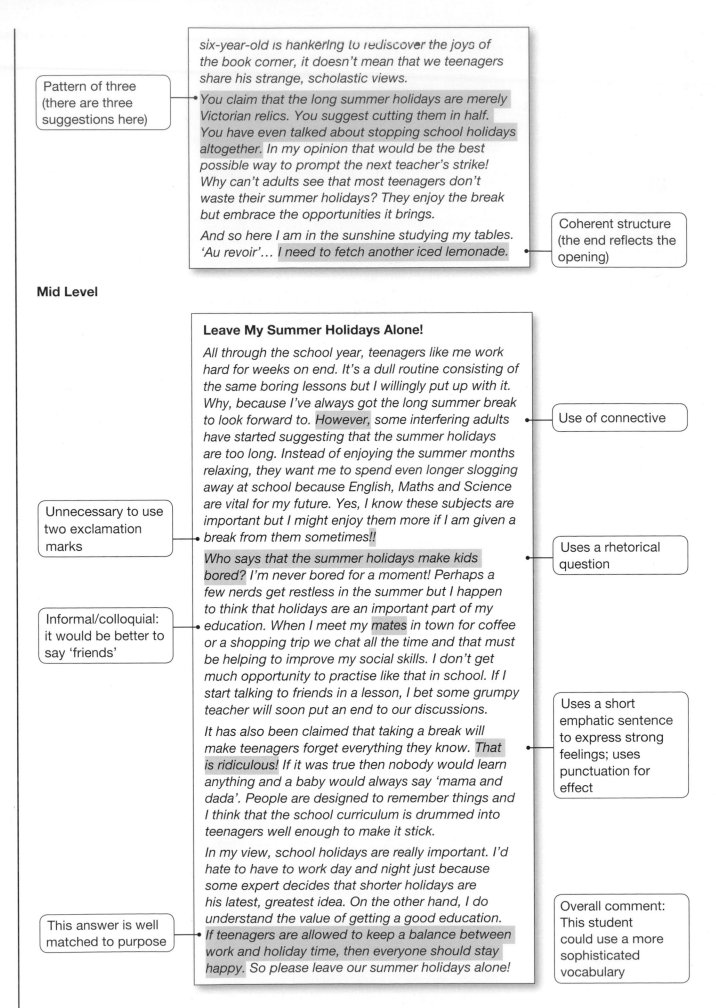

Pattern of three (there are three suggestions here)

six-year-old is hankering to rediscover the joys of the book corner, it doesn't mean that we teenagers share his strange, scholastic views.

You claim that the long summer holidays are merely Victorian relics. You suggest cutting them in half. You have even talked about stopping school holidays altogether. In my opinion that would be the best possible way to prompt the next teacher's strike! Why can't adults see that most teenagers don't waste their summer holidays? They enjoy the break but embrace the opportunities it brings.

And so here I am in the sunshine studying my tables. 'Au revoir'… I need to fetch another iced lemonade.

Coherent structure (the end reflects the opening)

Mid Level

Leave My Summer Holidays Alone!

All through the school year, teenagers like me work hard for weeks on end. It's a dull routine consisting of the same boring lessons but I willingly put up with it. Why, because I've always got the long summer break to look forward to. However, some interfering adults have started suggesting that the summer holidays are too long. Instead of enjoying the summer months relaxing, they want me to spend even longer slogging away at school because English, Maths and Science are vital for my future. Yes, I know these subjects are important but I might enjoy them more if I am given a break from them sometimes!!

Use of connective

Unnecessary to use two exclamation marks

Who says that the summer holidays make kids bored? I'm never bored for a moment! Perhaps a few nerds get restless in the summer but I happen to think that holidays are an important part of my education. When I meet my mates in town for coffee or a shopping trip we chat all the time and that must be helping to improve my social skills. I don't get much opportunity to practise like that in school. If I start talking to friends in a lesson, I bet some grumpy teacher will soon put an end to our discussions.

Uses a rhetorical question

Informal/colloquial: it would be better to say 'friends'

It has also been claimed that taking a break will make teenagers forget everything they know. That is ridiculous! If it was true then nobody would learn anything and a baby would always say 'mama and dada'. People are designed to remember things and I think that the school curriculum is drummed into teenagers well enough to make it stick.

Uses a short emphatic sentence to express strong feelings; uses punctuation for effect

In my view, school holidays are really important. I'd hate to have to work day and night just because some expert decides that shorter holidays are his latest, greatest idea. On the other hand, I do understand the value of getting a good education. If teenagers are allowed to keep a balance between work and holiday time, then everyone should stay happy. So please leave our summer holidays alone!

This answer is well matched to purpose

Overall comment: This student could use a more sophisticated vocabulary

Lower Level

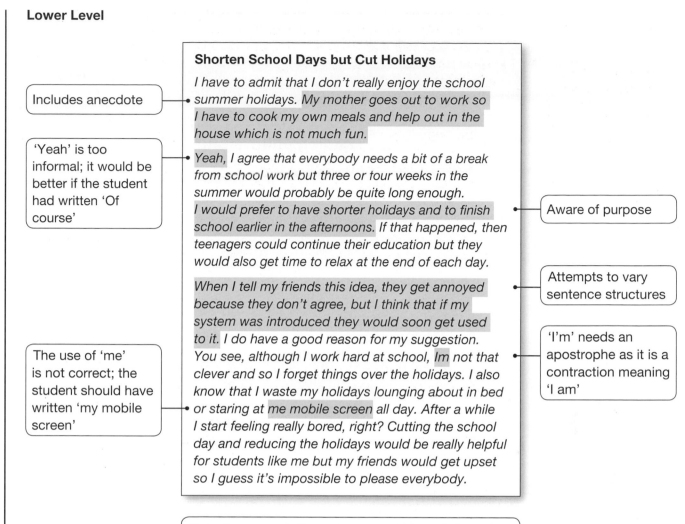

Includes anecdote

'Yeah' is too informal; it would be better if the student had written 'Of course'

The use of 'me' is not correct; the student should have written 'my mobile screen'

Shorten School Days but Cut Holidays

I have to admit that I don't really enjoy the school summer holidays. My mother goes out to work so I have to cook my own meals and help out in the house which is not much fun.

Yeah, I agree that everybody needs a bit of a break from school work but three or four weeks in the summer would probably be quite long enough. I would prefer to have shorter holidays and to finish school earlier in the afternoons. If that happened, then teenagers could continue their education but they would also get time to relax at the end of each day.

When I tell my friends this idea, they get annoyed because they don't agree, but I think that if my system was introduced they would soon get used to it. I do have a good reason for my suggestion. You see, although I work hard at school, Im not that clever and so I forget things over the holidays. I also know that I waste my holidays lounging about in bed or staring at me mobile screen all day. After a while I start feeling really bored, right? Cutting the school day and reducing the holidays would be really helpful for students like me but my friends would get upset so I guess it's impossible to please everybody.

Aware of purpose

Attempts to vary sentence structures

'I'm' needs an apostrophe as it is a contraction meaning 'I am'

Overall comment: This answer would benefit from the use of linguistic devices

PART THREE: YORK NOTES PRACTICE TEST TWO

Paper 1: Explorations in creative reading and writing

Time allowed: 1 hour 45 minutes

Materials

For this paper you must have:
- Source A – printed within the question paper.

Instructions

- Answer all questions.
- Answer the questions in the space provided, continuing onto a separate sheet if needed.
- Do all rough work in a notebook or on separate sheets of paper.
- You must refer to the sources provided.
- You should not use a dictionary.

Information

- The marks for questions are shown in brackets.
- The maximum mark for this paper is 80.
- There are 40 marks for Section A and 40 marks for Section B.
- You are reminded of the need for good English and clear presentation in your answers.
- The quality of your reading is assessed in Section A.
- The quality of your writing is assessed in Section B.

Advice

- You are advised to spend about 15 minutes reading through the source and all five questions you have to answer.
- You should make sure you leave sufficient time to check your answers.

Source A

This extract is taken from a short story called 'The Street of the Blank Wall' which was written by Jerome K. Jerome in 1906. In this extract the narrator is walking through the streets of London.

I had turned off from the Edgware Road into a street leading west, the atmosphere of which had appealed to me. It was a place of quiet houses standing behind little gardens. They had the usual names printed on the stuccoed[1] gateposts. The fading twilight was just sufficient to enable one to read them. There was a Laburnum Villa, and The Cedars, and a
5   Cairngorm, rising to the height of three storeys, with a curious little turret that branched out at the top, and was crowned with a conical roof, so that it looked as if wearing a witch's hat. Especially when two small windows just below the eaves sprang suddenly into light, and gave one the feeling of a pair of wicked eyes suddenly flashed upon one.

The street curved to the right, ending in an open space through which passed a canal
10   beneath a low arched bridge. There were still the same quiet houses behind their small gardens, and I watched for a while the lamplighter picking out the shape of the canal, that widened just above the bridge into a lake with an island in the middle. After that I must have wandered in a circle, for later on I found myself back in the same spot, though I do not suppose I had passed a dozen people on my way; and then I set to work to find my way back
15   to Paddington.

I thought I had taken the road by which I had come, but the half light must have deceived me. Not that it mattered. They had a lurking mystery about them, these silent streets with their suggestion of hushed movement behind drawn curtains, of whispered voices behind the flimsy walls. Occasionally there would escape the sound of laughter, suddenly stifled as it
20   seemed, and once the sudden cry of a child.

It was in a short street of semi-detached villas facing a high blank wall that, as I passed, I saw a blind move half-way up, revealing a woman's face. A gas lamp, the only one the street possessed, was nearly opposite. I thought at first it was the face of a girl, and then, as I looked again, it might have been the face of an old woman. One could not distinguish the
25   colouring. In any case, the cold, blue gaslight would have made it seem pallid.

The remarkable feature was the eyes. It might have been, of course, that they alone caught the light and held it, rendering them uncannily large and brilliant. Or it might have been that the rest of the face was small and delicate, out of all proportion to them. She may have seen me, for the blind was drawn down again, and I passed on.

30   There was no particular reason why, but the incident lingered with me. The sudden raising of the blind, as of the curtain of some small theatre, the barely furnished room coming dimly into view, and the woman standing there, close to the footlights, as to my fancy it seemed. And then the sudden ringing down of the curtain before the play had begun. I turned at the corner of the street. The blind had been drawn up again, and I saw again the slight, girlish figure silhouetted against the side panes of the bow window.

At the same moment a man knocked up against me. It was not his fault. I had stopped abruptly, not giving him time to avoid me. We both apologised, blaming the darkness. It may have been my fancy, but I had the feeling that, instead of going on his way, he had turned and was following me. I waited till the next corner, and then swung round on my heel. But there was no sign of him, and after a while I found myself back in the Edgware Road.

Glossary

stuccoed[1] – finished or decorated with fine plaster.

Section A: Reading

Answer **all** questions in this section.
You are advised to spend about 45 minutes on this section.

---

1 Read again the first part of the source, **lines 1 to 8**.

List **four** things from this part of the text about the street.

[4 marks]

1 _____

_____

2 _____

_____

3 _____

_____

4 _____

_____

2 Look in detail at this extract from **lines 9 to 20** of the source:

> The street curved to the right, ending in an open space through which passed a canal beneath a low arched bridge. There were still the same quiet houses behind their small gardens, and I watched for a while the lamplighter picking out the shape of the canal, that widened just above the bridge into a lake with an island in the middle. After that I must have wandered in a circle, for later on I found myself back in the same spot, though I do not suppose I had passed a dozen people on my way; and then I set to work to find my way back to Paddington.
>
> I thought I had taken the road by which I had come, but the half light must have deceived me. Not that it mattered. They had a lurking mystery about them, these silent streets with their suggestion of hushed movement behind drawn curtains, of whispered voices behind the flimsy walls. Occasionally there would escape the sound of laughter, suddenly stifled as it seemed, and once the sudden cry of a child.

How does the writer use language to create a mysterious atmosphere?

You could include the writer's choice of:

- words and phrases
- language features and techniques
- sentence forms.

[8 marks]

_____

_____

_____

_____

_____

_____

_____

_____

_____

_____

_____

_____

_____

_____

_____

_____

_____

_____

_____

_____

3 You now need to think about the **whole** of the **source.**

How has the writer structured the text to interest you as a reader?

You could write about:

- what the writer focuses your attention on at the beginning of the source
- how and why the writer changes this focus as the source develops
- any other structural features that interest you.

[8 marks]

4 Focus this part of your answer on the last part of the source, **from line 21 to the end.**

A student, having read this section of the text, said: 'The writer makes the woman's appearance at the window very mysterious. It makes me want to find out more about her.'

To what extent do you agree?

In your response, you could:
- write about your own impressions of the woman at the window
- evaluate how the writer has created these impressions
- support your opinions with references to the text.

[20 marks]

_____

_____

_____

_____

_____

_____

_____

_____

_____

_____

_____

_____

_____

_____

_____

_____

_____

_____

_____

_____

_____

Section B: Writing

You are advised to spend about 45 minutes on this section.

Write in full sentences.

You are reminded of the need to plan your answer.

You should leave enough time to check your work at the end.

---

5 You are going to enter a creative writing competition.

Your entry will be judged by a panel of people of your own age.

Either: Write a description suggested by this picture:

Or:

Write the opening part of a story that begins with somebody looking out of a window.

(24 marks for content and organisation
16 marks for technical accuracy)

[40 marks]

END OF QUESTIONS

Paper 2: Writers' viewpoints and perspectives

Time allowed: 1 hour 45 minutes

Materials

For this paper you must have:

■ Source A and Source B – which are located on pages 65–7.

Instructions

■ Answer all questions.
■ Answer the questions in the space provided, continuing onto a separate sheet if needed.
■ Do all rough work in a notebook or on separate sheets of paper.
■ You must refer to the Sources provided.
■ You should not use a dictionary.

Information

■ The marks for questions are shown in brackets.
■ The maximum mark for this paper is 80.
■ There are 40 marks for Section A and 40 marks for Section B.
■ You are reminded of the need for good English and clear presentation in your answers.
■ The quality of your reading is assessed in Section A.
■ The quality of your writing is assessed in Section B.

Advice

■ You are advised to spend about 15 minutes reading through the Sources and all five questions you have to answer.
■ You should make sure you leave sufficient time to check your answers.

Source A – 21st Century non-fiction

This Source is an extract from an anonymous article written for *The Guardian* by a gardener.

The secret life of a gardener: backache, stroppy clients and know-alls – but I love it

The Guardian, Monday 4 July 2016 (theguardian.com)

My client came tottering across the vast expanse of carefully striped lawn in a pair of heels that probably cost more than I make in a week. I stopped planting the wrong plant in the wrong spot that she had insisted upon, and awaited her arrival.

'I'm going out now,' she said, suspiciously eyeing up the hole I'd dug. 'I won't be able to pay
5   you today unless you can come back around eight tonight? I don't have any cash.'

She hadn't paid me for the last four weeks but I assured her it was OK, and she could pay me next time. She nodded and waved her hand dismissively. 'Can you also check the gutter outside the study window. I think it's leaking.'

I explained that I was a landscape gardener and I didn't really do that sort of thing. She
10   stared straight through me: 'Just make sure there aren't any leaves in there blocking the drainpipe. Maybe check the window frame too. There are also those little yellow leaves on the driveway again. Make sure you get rid of them and then straighten the gravel.'

She then slid on her large designer sunglasses and turned to walk back across the lawn, unsteadily towards her brand new car.

15   You might read this and conclude that I don't like being a gardener, but nothing could be further from the truth. I retrained in my thirties and wouldn't trade it for any job in the world – other than Premiership footballer, obviously. After trying a wide variety of jobs and going through a couple of redundancies, I decided that I needed to find a job that I could settle into, and which was relatively recession proof. I figured grass never stops growing so there
20   would always be a call for gardeners.

There is nothing better than spending all your days outside in unloved places turning them into beautiful ones. I get an immense sense of satisfaction upon completing a big design job and seeing the delight on a client's face, knowing I have made them a garden they will treasure for years to come.

25   In my 15 years of gardening, I have dealt with people from all walks of life. But I have to say, the majority of the difficult clients tend to be very rich. They want absolute perfection in the least amount of time and for the very minimum price you can give them. They will argue over every last penny and even time your lunch break to make sure they are getting the utmost effort for their money.

30   Apart from the rich, the next most difficult client would have to be what I call the 'Gardeners' World gardener'. They are the enthusiastic amateurs who read gardening magazines and know all the Latin names but don't want to do the physical work. They hover over your shoulder at all times and direct operations, which can be very wearing for eight hours. On many an occasion I have been very close to snapping at them as they asked for the plant I
35   had already planted four times in different positions to be moved to yet another corner.

My dream client is one who allows me to get on with my work with little interference and a decent budget. These jobs are very rare but when one comes along I am very grateful and will often put in extra unbilled hours just for the joy of it.

Aside from the weather, one of the worst things about being a gardener is the constant
40   pulling of muscles, and backache. Not so long ago I did my back in and was in immense pain, but I still had to work. Unluckily, it was a week when I was building a small patio courtyard. I managed to get through moving three tons of sand and all the cobbles, thanks to a mixture of gritted teeth, strong tea and painkillers.

It is a rare day when I get up in the morning and can move freely: some mornings my fingers
45   are like claws and my back is so tight that I move like a robot. I don't think I will be able to garden for much longer. I am 45 years old and I would guess I have another seven or eight years at most before I am physically unable to complete jobs. I have no idea what I will do after that, but it will have to be something with no heavy lifting involved.

There is a constant worry about not being able to work because of injury or illness and the
50   fact that we now have no real safety net in this country for people like myself.

As a gardener, downturns don't affect me as much as you might think. Of course there is some drop-off at the lower end of the business, but the people I mostly work for are recession proof and have too much land for them to ever take care of themselves. But I am a positive person and I think I have more to contribute to the world than my biceps and a
55   knowledge of turfing.

Source B – 19th Century literary non-fiction

This Source is taken from a letter written by the artist Sir John Everett Millais who lived from 1829–1896. In this letter he is writing to a man called Mr Combe about a stressful week at work.

---

83 Gower Street, December 16, 1852

My Dear Mr Combe,

Instead of going to a musical party with my father and brother, I will write you something of my doings. I have a headache and feel as tired as if I had walked twenty miles, from the
5 anxiety I have undergone this last fortnight.

All the morning I have been drawing a dog, which in unquietness is only to be surpassed by a child. Both of these animals I am trying to paint daily, and certainly nothing can exceed the trial of patience they occasion. The child screams upon entering the room, and when forcibly held in its mother's arms struggles with such successful obstinacy that I cannot
10 begin my work until exhaustion comes on, which generally appears when daylight disappears. A minute's quiet is out of the question. The only opportunity I have had was one evening, when it fell asleep just in the position I desired. Imagine looking forward to the day when next these two provoking models shall come! This is my only thought at night and upon waking in the morning.

15 When I suggest corporal punishment in times of extreme passion, the mother, after reminding me that I am not a father, breaks out into such reproofs as these: 'Poor dear! Was he bothered to sit to the gentleman? Precious daring! Is he to be tormented? No, my own one; no, my popsy, my flower, cherub,' etc., etc., dying away into kisses, when he (the baby) is placed upon his legs to run about my room and displace everything. Immediately he leaves
20 off crying, remarking that he sees a 'gee-gee' (pointing to a stag's head and antlers I have hung up), and would like to have one of my brushes.

This infant I could almost murder; but the dog I feel for, because he is not expected to understand. A strong man comes with it and bends him to my will, and all the while it looks as calm as a suffering martyr. I do more from this creature in a day than from the other in a week.

25 This year I hope you will come and see the produce of all this labour before the pictures go to the exhibition […]

Turn over for Section A

Section A: Reading

Answer **all** questions in this section.
You are advised to spend about 45 minutes on this section.

1 Read again the first part of **Source A, lines 1 to 14**.

Choose **four** statements below which are TRUE.

- Tick the boxes of the ones that you think are true.
- Choose a maximum of four statements.

[4 marks]

A The gardener has made the lawn look beautiful. ☐

B The gardener is inexperienced because he plants 'the wrong plant in the wrong spot'. ☐

C The client is not rich enough to pay the gardener for his work. ☐

D The client seems to doubt the gardener's abilities. ☐

E The gardener agrees to clear the drainpipe for his client. ☐

F The client listens carefully when the gardener explains his role. ☐

G The gardener is told to do several inappropriate jobs. ☐

H The gardener has no opportunity to discuss the suggested jobs with his client. ☐

2 You need to refer to **Source A** and **Source B** for this question:

Use details from **both** Sources. Write a summary of the differences between the problems that these writers face at work.

[8 marks]

_____

_____

_____

_____

_____

_____

_____

_____

_____

_____

_____

_____

_____

_____

_____

_____

_____

_____

_____

_____

_____

_____

_____

_____

_____

_____

3 You now need to refer **only** to **Source B**, the letter by Millais.

How does Millais use language to suggest that his work makes him feel stressed?

[12 marks]

Paper 2: Writers' viewpoints and perspectives

4 For this question, you need to refer to the **whole of Source A** together with **Source B**.

Compare how the two writers convey their attitudes towards their clients.

In your answer, you could:

- compare their different attitudes
- compare the methods they use to convey their attitudes
- support your ideas with references to both texts.

[16 marks]

_____

_____

_____

_____

_____

_____

_____

_____

_____

_____

_____

_____

_____

_____

_____

_____

_____

_____

_____

_____

_____

_____

_____

72

Section B: Writing

You are advised to spend about 45 minutes on this section.
Write in full sentences.
You are reminded of the need to plan your answer.
You should leave enough time to check your work at the end.

5 You have read an article in a broadsheet newspaper which states 'Becoming self-employed or running one's own business is the best option for young people in the future.'

Write a letter to the editor of the paper in which you argue for or against this viewpoint.

(24 marks for content and organisation
16 marks for technical accuracy)

[40 marks]

END OF QUESTIONS

Answers and sample responses

Paper 1: Section A

1 (AO1)

Any four or more answers from the following:

- The street was 'leading west'.
- It was 'a place of quiet houses'.
- The houses were 'standing behind little gardens'.
- The house names were 'printed on the stuccoed gateposts'.
- The house names seemed 'usual'.
- Three of the houses were called 'Laburnum Villa', 'The Cedars' and 'Cairngorm'.
- Cairngorm had a turret 'crowned with a conical roof' which resembled a witch's hat.

2 (AO2)

Possible answers

- The silence of the atmosphere is emphasised by the adjective 'quiet'.
- The writer encourages readers to share the narrator's journey by describing his route in detail using a long sentence to reflect the way that the road 'curved to the right, ending in an open space through which passed a canal beneath a low arched bridge'.
- The adjective 'low' implies a sense of restriction.
- We know it is almost dark because the lamplighter is 'picking out the shape of the canal'. Night is often used as a mysterious setting for sinister events.
- The island in the middle of the lake may be a symbol of isolation.
- This sense of isolation is reinforced when the narrator states, 'I do not suppose I passed a dozen people'. This implies that the streets were almost empty.
- The narrator seems lost as he 'wandered in a circle'. The verb 'wandered' suggests disorientation or a lack of certainty.
- When the narrator states, 'the half light must have deceived me' the verb 'deceived' suggests trickery and the reference to 'half light' reminds us of the gloomy atmosphere.
- 'These silent streets' is an alliterative phrase which once again draws attention to the quietness that surrounds the narrator.
- The noun 'mystery' (the focus of this question) is used directly in the text in the phrase 'lurking mystery'.
- 'Lurking' is usually associated with guilt, secrecy or threat.
- The phrase 'suggestion of hushed movement'

reinforces the silence again through 'hushed', and the fact that these movements take place 'behind drawn curtains' implies secrecy and mystery.

- The phrase 'whispered voices behind the flimsy walls' uses sibilance to reflect the sound of the whispering itself.
- The adjective 'flimsy' suggests something insubstantial and easily torn, implying vulnerability.
- The verb 'stifled' has connotations of constraint or restriction.
- Since the sound of laughter is 'suddenly stifled' the narrator suggests that joy was inappropriate in this setting.
- The adjective 'sudden' in 'sudden cry of a child' implies something unexpected which might shock the narrator.
- The 'cry of a child' suggests negative emotion such as sorrow or pain.

Sample student responses

Level	Skills descriptors
Higher	Shows detailed and perceptive understanding of *language*: You select a very well-chosen range of details from the text. You analyse the effects of the writer's choices of *language*. You make sophisticated use of accurate terminology.
Mid	Shows clear understanding of *language*: You select a relevant range of details from the text. You clearly explain the effects of the writer's choices of *language*. You use accurate terminology.

Higher Level

This extract opens with an extended descriptive sentence. This is designed to encourage readers to become imaginatively involved in the narrator's journey along the road that 'curved to the right'. The adjective 'low', describing the 'arched bridge', implies a sense of restriction and limitation which is further reinforced by additional adjectives throughout the text, such as 'small', 'stifled', 'hushed' and 'quiet'. Furthermore, the writer's reference to 'quiet houses' and 'hushed movement' suggests an unnatural or forced silence which enhances the mystery of this setting.

We know that it is nearly night because the lamplighter is 'picking out the shape of the canal'. The verb 'deceived' used in 'the half light must have deceived me' has connotations of trickery or foul play. Furthermore, night and darkness are often used as the backdrop for mysterious stories. Moreover, the narrator seems to be lost since the verb 'wandered' implies his lack of certainty or direction.

The writer develops the reader's awareness of the strange, hushed atmosphere surrounding the narrator through using alliteration in the adjective noun combination 'silent streets'. In addition, sibilance is apparent in the phrase 'whispered voices behind flimsy walls' and the words themselves suggest a whispering sound. Furthermore, the 'sudden cry of a child' seems shocking since the adjective 'sudden' implies something unexpected and a cry is usually associated with sorrow or suffering.

Mid Level

In this extract the writer creates a hushed atmosphere when he refers to 'the same quiet houses'. The use of the adjective 'quiet' emphasises the silence of this place. A similar idea is repeated later when the writer makes reference to 'these silent streets'. The adjective and noun in 'silent streets' both begin with 's' so this is alliteration and the effect is a sort of whispering sound. This sound could be connected to the idea of 'whispered voices behind flimsy curtains' which makes us imagine that this is the kind of place where people are hiding away and watching the man as he wanders around. I can also infer that he is lost because he is walking in 'a circle'.

The scene takes place at night because the narrator says, 'the half light must have deceived me'. I think this reference to 'half light' makes the setting seem gloomy and when he writes 'deceived me' it sounds suspicious. We are also aware that it is night when he mentions the lamplighter. The setting seems sinister because of the 'sudden cry of a child'. This child sounds unhappy and if the cry was 'sudden' it probably startled the narrator.

3 (AO2)

Possible answers

- This text has a circular structure since it begins and ends with references to the Edgware Road. This is appropriate as the man 'must have wandered in a circle'.
- The overall focus of this piece moves from an observation of the neighbourhood to a very specific focus on the woman's appearance at the window until the narrator is jolted back to reality when a man bumps into him.
- The first time the focus narrows is in the opening paragraph where the narrator examines the houses in general and then focuses in on the house called Cairngorm.

- This house is described in more detail than the others and its description has sinister associations since it has a tower on top and the conical roof is compared to a witch's hat.
- There is a particular focus on two small windows of this house which looked like 'wicked eyes'. This possibly foreshadows the later episode where the woman's eyes are closely observed.
- The writer encourages us to follow the narrator's journey since we are given directions to make us aware of his path: 'I had turned off' and 'The street curved to the right'.
- Each of the first three paragraphs begins with a sentence about his route.
- Although we are giving some information about the canal, which passed 'beneath a low arched bridge' and 'widened just above the bridge', the writer does not provide much detailed description, suggesting that the narrator is passing by rather than examining anything carefully at this point in the text.
- Throughout this episode the narrator feels that he is under scrutiny and the writer highlights this throughout the text. In the first paragraph the windows on the strange house 'gave one the feeling of a pair of wicked eyes suddenly flashed upon one'. Later there is a very close focus on the eyes of the woman at the window who 'may have seen me' and finally we are told that the man who bumped into the narrator was possibly 'following me'.
- The focus of the piece narrows down completely when the narrator notices the woman. Details about her and her surroundings are gradually revealed.
- This woman is given three paragraphs of the text, suggesting her importance.
- At first the focus on the woman is indistinct as her age is unclear: 'I thought at first it was the face of a girl, and then, as I looked again, it might have been the face of an old woman'.
- Later more details are provided when we are told that she was illuminated by 'cold, blue gaslight' and finally the writer zooms right in on her eyes which were 'uncannily large and brilliant'.
- However, a totally clear picture of this woman is never given so she remains mysterious.
- After the narrator leaves the woman another whole paragraph is devoted to examining her appearance. This means that the reader's attention is also kept focused on the woman for longer, echoing how 'the incident lingered' with the narrator.
- When a man bumps into the narrator the focus of the text shifts abruptly away from the window.
- The extract closes 'back in the Edgware Road', completing its circular structure.

Sample student responses

Level	Skills descriptors
Higher	Shows detailed and perceptive understanding of *structural* features: You select a very well-chosen range of examples. You analyse the effects of these features. You refer to them by making sophisticated use of accurate terminology.
Mid	Shows clear understanding of *structural* features: You select a range of relevant examples. You refer to them by making clear use of accurate terminology.

Higher Level

This text, about a man who 'must have wandered in a circle' has a circular structure since it begins and ends with references to the Edgware Road. Throughout this episode, the writer encourages readers to accompany the narrator on his journey. For this reason, each of the first three paragraphs begins with directional information, such as informing readers that the 'street curved to the right'.

The text is structured so that it follows the narrator's gaze as it moves from the general, to the specific, and back again. Early on there is a moment when the man focuses on a row of 'quiet houses' and then goes on to examine one specific house in this row. To reflect this, the writer begins with a wide focus on this building's general construction, then closes in on the conical roof which resembled 'a witch's hat'. Finally, the reader's attention is drawn to its strange eyelike windows, which foreshadow other moments yet to come when the man feels under scrutiny.

Around the middle of this extract, the writer places its main event: a mysterious woman is seen illuminated at a window. At first she is indistinct, as even her age seems uncertain, but soon the writer focuses in on various mysterious details such as her pale face illuminated by the 'cold blue gaslight' and her eyes shining 'uncannily large and brilliant'. However, although such specific information is provided, the writer's focus always remains slightly blurred to resemble the narrator's confusion about what he is seeing.

The narrator claims that 'the incident lingered with me' and this is reflected in the text, which allows the woman to feature in another reflective paragraph after the narrator has passed by. Reality only returns when

a stranger bumps into the narrator, and here the text shifts away from the window to finish 'back in the Edgware Road', bringing the episode full circle.

Mid Level

In his first paragraph the writer provides readers with a view of the setting as we are told 'It was a place of quiet houses'. He then closes in on one particular house which has a roof like a witch's hat and windows like 'wicked eyes'.

His focus widens again to give us a general description of the canal scene but then it narrows down towards the woman at the window. At first the focus on this woman is unclear as we are not told exactly what she looks like ('I thought at first it was the face of a girl, and then, as I looked again, it might have been the face of an old woman') but later on the writer draws a bit closer to reveal more information and eventually readers learn that she has a 'slight, girlish figure'.

At the end of this piece somebody bumps into the narrator and that stops him thinking about the woman so at this stage the writer shifts attention back to the street.

4 (AO4)

Possible answers

- The writer makes the woman seems mysterious because of the way she opens and closes the blind, allowing us only brief glimpses of her life.
- Near the beginning of the episode we are told that the narrator saw 'a blind move half-way up'. The fact that it is only half-way up is used to suggest that there is something being hidden.
- We are given the sense that the woman wants to observe the narrator without him observing her because once she is sure he is out of sight she opens the blind again.
- We want to know more about this woman when certain details about her are not revealed, such as her colouring which 'One could not distinguish'.
- Even her age is left uncertain because the narrator thought he saw 'the face of a girl, and then' when he looked again 'it might have been the face of an old woman'.
- The writer implies that the woman could be vulnerable as a girl may be young and naïve and an old woman may be frail.
- This image of her frailty is supported when we are told that 'the face was small and delicate' and that she has a 'slight, girlish figure'. Both 'delicate' and 'slight' suggest fragility.
- The mystery of the piece is enhanced by the reference to a strange gas light that falls across the woman's face. This concept of cold, blue light seems sinister or ghostly.

- The writer uses the modal verbs 'might' and 'may' to suggest possibilities. He repeats 'it might have been …' twice to draw attention to this uncertainty and also explains that 'she may have seen me'.
- The narrator says, 'The remarkable feature was the eyes.' The word 'remarkable' implies that there was something unusual about them. This intrigues us.
- We learn that the eyes 'caught the light and held it, rendering them uncannily large and brilliant'. The idea of large eyes might seem sinister or ghostly.
- The writer uses a theatrical image when he refers to 'The sudden raising of the blind, as of the curtain of some small theatre'. This image is developed in the line 'the woman standing there, close to the footlights'. A play is something unreal and removed from ordinary life.
- We are also told about 'the sudden ringing down of the curtain before the play had begun'. This implies that the narrator had missed some part of the action and therefore enhances the mystery.
- The narrator states, 'the incident lingered with me', which implies that the woman made a significant impression on him. This encourages us to think about it for longer too.
- The writer deliberately leaves some details about the house until the end of the episode, for example he mentions 'the barely furnished room' and 'the bow window'. This delay in revealing specific details about her home shrouds the woman's circumstances in mystery and makes the reader want to read on in order to discover more.

Sample student responses

Level	Skills descriptors
Higher	Shows perceptive and detailed evaluation: You select a very well-chosen range of details from the text. You provide a detailed critical evaluation of the effect(s) on the reader. You show perceptive understanding of the writer's methods. You develop a convincing and critical response to the statement in the question.
Mid	Shows clear and relevant evaluation: You select a relevant range of details from the text. You clearly evaluate the effect(s) on the reader. You show a clear understanding of the writer's methods. You make a clear and relevant response to the statement in the question.

Higher Level

I agree with the student's statement: this woman seems to be shrouded in mystery since the writer only reveals her in fleeting glimpses as she opens and closes the blind. Even when she does appear, her blind only moves 'half-way up', so she remains partly obscured. This sense of partial concealment is developed through the narrator's inability to tell if she is a 'girl' or an 'old woman' and modal verbs such as 'might have been' and 'may have seen me' are cleverly used to enhance the impression of uncertainty.

This woman also seems mysterious because Jerome K. Jerome makes her appear ghostly. We learn that her face is illuminated by 'cold, blue gaslight' which 'would have made it seem pallid'. This image is then combined with a startling description of her 'remarkable' eyes which 'caught the light and held it, rendering them uncannily large and brilliant'. These eyes seem unnatural or unworldly, increasing the sense of mystery surrounding the woman.

Jerome intrigues his readers further by introducing a theatrical image comparing the woman's window blind to 'the curtain of some small theatre'. The woman is observed 'standing there, close to the footlights', which are specifically used on a stage. There is a suggestion that the narrator has missed some important part of the action since the woman closed the blind again 'before the play had begun'. Readers are therefore encouraged to wonder what her strange performance is really about and they, like the student, long 'to find out more' about the woman who has made such a brief but tantalising appearance.

Mid Level

I agree with the student – I want to find out more about the woman. The writer makes her seem like an actress in a play when she opens and closes her blind like 'the curtain of some small theatre'. This is interesting because in a play you learn more about the characters, but we don't learn a lot about this woman.

The writer makes the woman mysterious by giving us a few details about her face, such as her 'remarkable eyes'. This makes me imagine her eyes being huge and glowing in the 'blue gaslight' which seems eerie. However, the writer never tells us exactly what the woman looks like. The narrator says, 'at first it was the face of a girl, and then, […] it might have been the face of an old woman'. This is unclear and makes me want to know more.

I think the writer wants us to think that woman is poor because her house is 'barely furnished'. I get the impression she has had a hard life and I want to know more.

Paper 1: Section B

5 (AO5) (AO6)

Level	Skills descriptors
Higher	**Content (AO5)** Your writing is confidently matched to the purpose of the task. Your register is convincing and compelling to the audience. You use an extensive and ambitious vocabulary. Your work is well crafted. You make excellent use of linguistic devices. **Organisation (AO5)** Your writing is compelling. You make varied and inventive use of structural features. You include a range of convincing and complex ideas. Your paragraphs are linked fluently. **Technical Accuracy (AO6)** Your sentences are well defined and consistently accurate. You use a range of punctuation with a high level of accuracy. You use a full range of appropriate sentence forms for effect. You use Standard English consistently and appropriately. Your grammar is excellent. Your spelling is highly accurate, including the spelling of ambitious vocabulary.
Mid	**Content (AO5)** Your writing is generally well matched to the purpose of the task. Your register is generally matched to the audience. Your vocabulary is chosen for effect and you make some sophisticated word choices. You use linguistic devices successfully. **Organisation (AO5)** Your writing is engaging. You make effective use of structural features. You use a range of clear, connected ideas. Your paragraphs are well linked. **Technical Accuracy (AO6)** Your sentences are securely defined and mostly accurate. You use a range of punctuation mostly with success. You use a variety of sentence forms for effect. You use Standard English appropriately. Your grammar is good. Your spelling is generally accurate, including the spelling of complex and irregular words.
Lower	**Content (AO5)** Your writing is sometimes matched to the purpose of the task. You try to match your register (level of formality) to the audience. You make an attempt to vary your vocabulary. You make some use of linguistic devices. **Organisation (AO5)** Some of your writing is clear. You use some structural features. You include a variety of linked and relevant ideas. You use paragraphs and make some use of discourse markers.

(continued on the next page)

Lower (continued)	**Technical Accuracy (AO6)** Most of your sentences are correctly defined. You show some control of a range of punctuation. You try to use a variety of sentence forms. You mostly use Standard English. Some of your grammar is correct. Your work includes some accurate spelling of more complex words.

Write a description suggested by the picture on page 60.

Sample student responses

Higher Level

Use of a compound sentence (variety of sentence structures; use of literary device (personification in 'shoulders of factories')

Clever use of personification to add interest

This is a place of silence. Yellow-brown buildings tower over the street, their bricks discoloured by toxic smoke. Yesterday's snow clings to pavements. Locked shutters prohibit entry. A white moon shines and clouds skulk across the shoulders of factories.

To the left, two street lamps project warm light onto empty windows. Their illusion of cosiness is just a foolish fancy. To the right, a metal balcony hangs over a gate. It lurks near the place where a graffiti artist made his mark in bold, oriental swirls. Nearby, a street sign stands upright in uncomfortable snow shoes.

The little grey road has thrown off her snow using grease and the passing feet of strangers. She mocks those doorsteps that still lie stifled.

On the horizon, a warehouse stands guard, one eye alight with a faint reflection of the moon. This is a place of silence.

Short sentences are used to convey a tense atmosphere

Creates a strong sense of place ('To the left' / 'To the right' / 'Nearby')

Coherent structure; the ending mirrors the opening

Mid Level

Could use a wider variety of sentence openings rather than repeating 'The'

The word 'paintwork' has been used later in the sentence. The student could have used 'tags' here instead

It is a cold night. Tall, brown buildings stand above the snow. Blue clouds float through the sky. The street is empty. The street lights shine across pavements. Piles of snow have been stacked up on these pavements and more snow sits on the slippery steps.

Above this scene a white moon casts its light. It reveals graffiti. Black and white spray paint have been used to spoil the paintwork. It makes this place look so unfriendly. Beside the graffiti door, a closed linen blind hangs as white as the snow. It is almost translucent, suggesting that there may be life going on behind it. But the street is totally deserted.

Uses visual details

Use of alliteration ('s')

Uses some sophisticated vocabulary

Lower Level

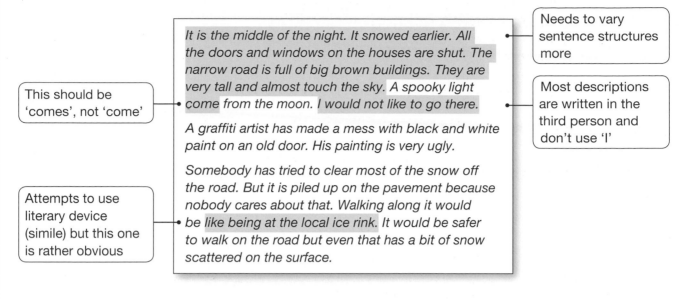

This should be 'comes', not 'come'

Attempts to use literary device (simile) but this one is rather obvious

> It is the middle of the night. It snowed earlier. All the doors and windows on the houses are shut. The narrow road is full of big brown buildings. They are very tall and almost touch the sky. A spooky light come from the moon. I would not like to go there.
>
> A graffiti artist has made a mess with black and white paint on an old door. His painting is very ugly.
>
> Somebody has tried to clear most of the snow off the road. But it is piled up on the pavement because nobody cares about that. Walking along it would be like being at the local ice rink. It would be safer to walk on the road but even that has a bit of snow scattered on the surface.

Needs to vary sentence structures more

Most descriptions are written in the third person and don't use 'I'

Write the opening part of a story that begins with somebody looking out of a window.

Higher Level

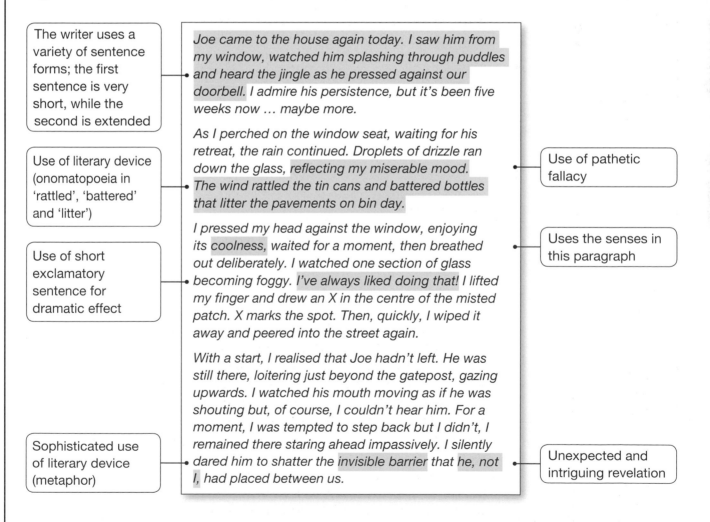

The writer uses a variety of sentence forms; the first sentence is very short, while the second is extended

Use of literary device (onomatopoeia in 'rattled', 'battered' and 'litter')

Use of short exclamatory sentence for dramatic effect

Sophisticated use of literary device (metaphor)

> Joe came to the house again today. I saw him from my window, watched him splashing through puddles and heard the jingle as he pressed against our doorbell. I admire his persistence, but it's been five weeks now … maybe more.
>
> As I perched on the window seat, waiting for his retreat, the rain continued. Droplets of drizzle ran down the glass, reflecting my miserable mood. The wind rattled the tin cans and battered bottles that litter the pavements on bin day.
>
> I pressed my head against the window, enjoying its coolness, waited for a moment, then breathed out deliberately. I watched one section of glass becoming foggy. I've always liked doing that! I lifted my finger and drew an X in the centre of the misted patch. X marks the spot. Then, quickly, I wiped it away and peered into the street again.
>
> With a start, I realised that Joe hadn't left. He was still there, loitering just beyond the gatepost, gazing upwards. I watched his mouth moving as if he was shouting but, of course, I couldn't hear him. For a moment, I was tempted to step back but I didn't, I remained there staring ahead impassively. I silently dared him to shatter the invisible barrier that he, not I, had placed between us.

Use of pathetic fallacy

Uses the senses in this paragraph

Unexpected and intriguing revelation

Mid Level

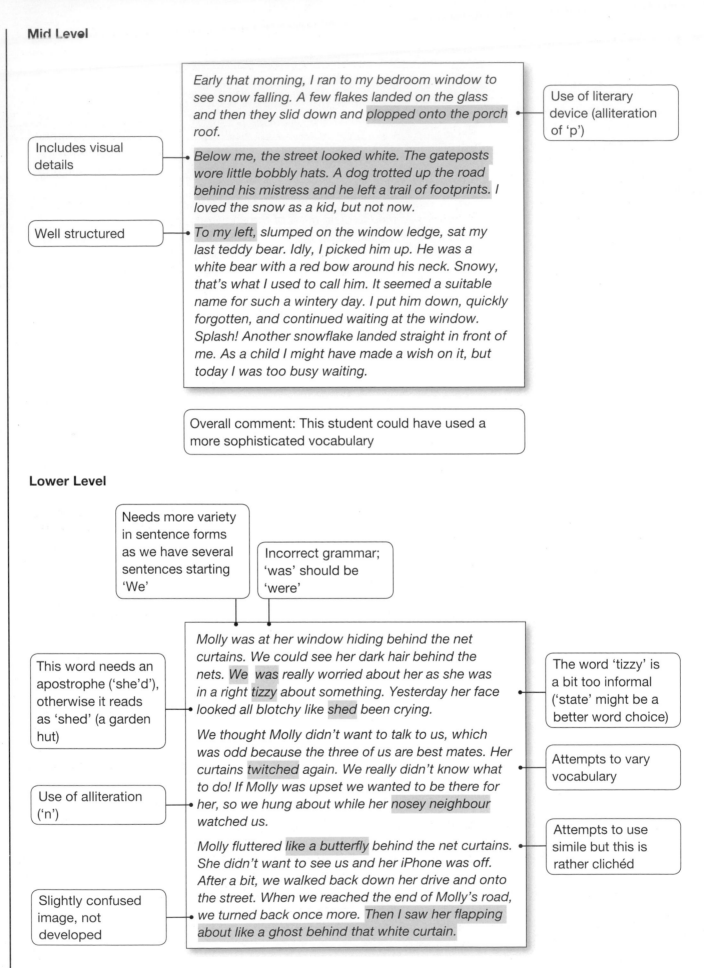

Includes visual details

Well structured

Early that morning, I ran to my bedroom window to see snow falling. A few flakes landed on the glass and then they slid down and plopped onto the porch roof.

Below me, the street looked white. The gateposts wore little bobbly hats. A dog trotted up the road behind his mistress and he left a trail of footprints. I loved the snow as a kid, but not now.

To my left, slumped on the window ledge, sat my last teddy bear. Idly, I picked him up. He was a white bear with a red bow around his neck. Snowy, that's what I used to call him. It seemed a suitable name for such a wintery day. I put him down, quickly forgotten, and continued waiting at the window. Splash! Another snowflake landed straight in front of me. As a child I might have made a wish on it, but today I was too busy waiting.

Use of literary device (alliteration of 'p')

Overall comment: This student could have used a more sophisticated vocabulary

Lower Level

Needs more variety in sentence forms as we have several sentences starting 'We'

Incorrect grammar; 'was' should be 'were'

This word needs an apostrophe ('she'd'), otherwise it reads as 'shed' (a garden hut)

Use of alliteration ('n')

Slightly confused image, not developed

Molly was at her window hiding behind the net curtains. We could see her dark hair behind the nets. We was really worried about her as she was in a right tizzy about something. Yesterday her face looked all blotchy like shed been crying.

We thought Molly didn't want to talk to us, which was odd because the three of us are best mates. Her curtains twitched again. We really didn't know what to do! If Molly was upset we wanted to be there for her, so we hung about while her nosey neighbour watched us.

Molly fluttered like a butterfly behind the net curtains. She didn't want to see us and her iPhone was off. After a bit, we walked back down her drive and onto the street. When we reached the end of Molly's road, we turned back once more. Then I saw her flapping about like a ghost behind that white curtain.

The word 'tizzy' is a bit too informal ('state' might be a better word choice)

Attempts to vary vocabulary

Attempts to use simile but this is rather clichéd

Paper 2: Section A

1 (AO1)

A   The gardener has made the lawn look beautiful. (T)
B   The gardener is inexperienced because he plants 'the wrong plant in the wrong spot'. (F)
C   The client is not rich enough to pay the gardener for his work. (F)
D   The client seems to doubt the gardener's abilities. (T)
E   The gardener agrees to clear the drainpipe for his client. (F)
F   The client listens carefully when the gardener explains his role. (F)
G   The gardener is told to do several inappropriate jobs. (T)
H   The gardener has no opportunity to discuss the suggested jobs with his client. (T)

2 (AO1)

Possible answers

Problems associated with work in Source A by the gardener

- The gardener hasn't been paid for 'four weeks'.
- He is given work to do that is not appropriate to his role and has to explain 'I didn't really do that sort of thing'.
- Amateur gardeners hover over his shoulder. They 'know all the Latin names but don't want to do the physical work'.
- He does not always feel trusted and the client looks at his work 'suspiciously'.
- He is asked to plant 'the wrong plant in the wrong spot' by his client.
- The weather can cause him difficulties.
- He gets various aches and pains and his back gets 'so tight that I move like a robot'.
- He has a 'constant worry' that he may not be able to work due to age, illness or injury.

Problems associated with work in Source B by Millais

- He has difficult and 'provoking' models to work with.
- The child only settles down when asleep and it struggles and 'screams'.
- He gets no peace and even a minute of 'quiet is out of the question'.
- He worries about his work 'at night and upon waking'.
- The child's mother does not seem to understand his viewpoint and reminds him that he is 'not a father'.
- His materials get disturbed when the child is allowed to 'run about' and 'displace everything'.

- He gets a headache from work stress and feels as if he had 'walked twenty miles' after working with the dog and the child.

Sample student responses

Level	Skills descriptors
Higher	Shows perceptive synthesis and interpretation of both texts: You select well-chosen details from the texts. These details are relevant to the focus of the question. You make perceptive inferences from both texts. Your statements show perceptive differences between texts.
Mid	Shows clear synthesis and interpretation of both texts: You select clear details from the texts. These details are relevant to the focus of the question. You make clear inferences from both texts. Your statements show clear differences between texts.

Higher Level

Both the gardener and Millais encounter difficulties at work and many of their problems arise from the people they work with. The gardener sometimes has to wait for payment for as long as 'four weeks' or else he is expected to hang around until the evening to collect his money. Millais also has to work late for a different reason: he has to wait for his troublesome child model to fall asleep.

Both writers are experts and yet they are not understood or trusted. The gardener's work is eyed 'suspiciously' and he is instructed to 'plant the wrong plant in the wrong spot'. He is also asked to move plants several times by the 'enthusiastic amateurs' who hover over his shoulder. Similarly, Millais gets no support from the child's mother who reminds him that he is 'not a father' and allows her child to run about and 'displace everything'.

Millais and the gardener both face various symptoms as a result of their work. The gardener's work is physical so he suffers from aches and pains and has a 'constant worry about not being able to work' due to injury or ill-health. Millais suffers mentally as he can't stop thinking about his two 'provoking models'. As a result of this anxiety he gets a headache and feels as if he had 'walked twenty miles'.

Mid Level

Millais and the gardener both face problems at work. The gardener has to deal with difficult clients who don't pay him on time and one lady makes him clear the gutter even though he is a landscape gardener. On the other hand, Millais has to work with a dog, a screaming child and the child's annoying mother. The young child seems particularly irritating because he won't settle down and the mother makes things worse by letting him run about and disturb everything.

The gardener gets a lot of aches and pains from his work and so he is worried about getting old and not being able to work any more. Millais gets a headache from anxiety and he can't ever relax because he worries about his models 'at night and upon waking in the morning'.

3 (AO2)

Possible answers

- The noun 'anxiety' implies nervousness, worry or unease and these are all stress factors.
- A headache (noun) is a common stress symptom.
- Millais says he feels 'as tired as if I had walked twenty miles'. This image implies that he is suffering physically due to his stress.
- The combination of 'nothing' with the verb 'exceed' in the phrase 'nothing can exceed the trial of patience they occasion' suggests that Millais is facing the worst possible provocation.
- The noun 'patience' in 'trial of patience' relates to his ability to deal with problems, but here he is implying that his patience is being tested.
- The combination of the adjective 'successful' with the noun 'obstinacy' seems unusual as obstinacy is a negative trait (implying stubbornness) while 'successful' is usually associated with accomplishment or victory. This juxtaposition could be designed to suggest that Millais believes that the child is deliberately causing him stress.
- Millais feels that even a minute of quiet is 'out of the question', which means it is impossible to relax – again implying that he is facing extreme conditions.
- The combination of the adjective 'extreme' with the noun 'passion' (meaning strong emotion) highlights the strength of his feelings.
- Millais is so stressed that he would like to resort to violence and he mentions 'corporal punishment', which means beating or smacking.
- Millais calls his models 'provoking', an adjective which means causing irritation or giving rise to strong emotions.
- Millais is constantly thinking about his problems 'at night and upon waking in the morning', which shows that he cannot rest or relax even when he is not painting.

- The adjective 'only' in 'my only thought' implies he is completely preoccupied with his models.
- The adverb 'almost' slightly qualifies the noun 'murder' which would otherwise imply that Millais is so stressed that he wants to kill the child.
- The fact that Millais moves on from a reference to 'corporal punishment' to a reference to 'murder' could suggest that his stress levels are rising.

Sample student responses

Level	Skills descriptors
Higher	Shows detailed and perceptive understanding of *language*: You select a range of well-chosen details from the text. You analyse the effects of the writer's choices of *language*. You make sophisticated and accurate use of terminology.
Mid	Shows clear understanding of *language*: You select a range of relevant details from the text. You clearly explain the effects of the writer's choices of *language*. You make clear and accurate use of terminology.

Higher Level

The purpose of Millais's letter is clearly to share his feelings with Mr Combe. He uses the noun 'anxiety' in the first paragraph and claims that he is suffering from a headache. Millais also feels as if he had 'walked twenty miles', which implies that he is exhausted by his work.

Throughout his letter Millais uses language which implies that he is being pushed to extremes by his models, such as 'nothing can exceed the trial of patience they occasion' and 'A minute's quiet is out of the question.' He even implies that the child is deliberately provoking him when he refers to it struggling with 'successful obstinacy'. Here the deliberate juxtaposition of the positive adjective 'successful' with the noun 'obstinacy' (implying stubbornness) implies that Millais is very annoyed by the infant.

His stress can also be observed when he writes about his 'extreme passion'. Here the noun 'passion' refers to a strong emotion (possibly anger) and the combination of the adjective 'extreme' with this noun once again implies a strong emotional reaction. Millais's stress appears to rise as he is forced to spend more time with the child. Initially, he suggests 'corporal punishment' but then he goes on to contemplate 'murder' although he does qualify this with the adverb 'almost' when he explains that he could 'almost murder' the infant.

It is evident that Millais is stressed because he is constantly preoccupied with his models and he thinks about them 'at night and upon waking in the morning'. This implies that they are always troubling him, an idea which is supported by the adjective 'only' when he claims they are his 'only' thought.

Mid Level

Millais tells Mr Coombe about how anxious he feels because of having to work with a young child and a dog. He claims that he has a 'headache' and this is clearly associated with stress. He also compares what he has endured with the experience of walking for twenty miles which could mean he is very tired.

Millais thinks about his models constantly 'at night and upon waking'. This makes me feel sympathy for him as it seems as though he can never relax because of them.

Millais calls the child and dog 'provoking models' and his choice of the word 'provoking' means that they are really irritating him. He gets so stressed by the child that he feels 'extreme passion'. Here the adjective 'extreme' implies that he is in a very bad temper and this makes him suggest smacking the child. Later on he seems even more stressed, as he tells Mr Coombe that he is ready to 'almost murder' this child. Since he is tempted to kill it he must be feeling really stressed. Nobody would normally think of killing a little child.

4 (AO3)

Possible answers

- Both Millais and the gardener have difficult clients who cause them irritation.
- The gardener uses humour to reveal the nature of a rich client who is described as 'tottering' in her high heel shoes. This description makes her appear comic.
- He shows us that she is rich since her shoes 'cost more than I make in a week' and her car is 'brand new', which implies that he is annoyed that she hasn't paid him.
- Millais's letter is also amusing – but only to the reader, as he is clearly venting his irritation rather than using humour as a deliberate technique.

- He refers to both his models as 'provoking', implying that they make him angry.
- Both writers include some of the things that their clients say in order to reveal more about them.
- The rich woman speaks dismissively to the gardener and asks him to do inappropriate chores even after he explains that this is not his role.
- Millais tells Mr Coombe that the mother calls her child 'my popsy' and 'my flower' and other similar names. The pronoun 'my' is used as a declaration of her adoring, possessive love for her son.
- The writers both give alternative names to their clients.
- The gardener calls one type of client 'the Gardeners' World gardener'. This client knows the Latin names of plants but is not prepared to 'do the physical work'.
- Millais refers to the dog and child as 'these animals', implying that the child is no different from the dog.
- The structure of the texts is also significant.
- Millais begins with a bid for sympathy when he refers to his headache.
- The gardener initially gains sympathy through his anecdote about his rich client.
- Millais uses a similar technique when he dedicates a whole paragraph to the child.
- After these first critical portraits each writer creates another.
- The gardener tells us about enthusiastic amateurs who are constantly at his shoulder and Millais reveals how the child's mother gushes over her baby.
- Both writers are so irritated that they want to retaliate.
- The gardener explains that he gets 'very close to snapping' and Millais considers corporal punishment before admitting that he could 'almost murder' the child.
- Both writers suggest that their clients differ. Some are easier to work with.
- The gardener refers to a rare 'dream client'.
- Millais has some sympathy for the dog because there is a trainer who 'comes with it and bends it to my will'. He compares the dog favourably to the child.

Sample student responses

Level	Skills descriptors
Higher	Compares ideas and perspectives in a perceptive way: You analyse how writers' methods are used. You select a range of well-chosen supporting detail from both texts. You show a detailed understanding of the different ideas and perspectives in both texts.
Mid	Compares ideas and perspectives in a clear and relevant way: You explain clearly how writers' methods are used. You select relevant detail from both texts. You show a clear understanding of the different ideas and perspectives in both texts.

Higher Level

Both the gardener and Millais view certain clients as an irritation. The gardener reveals his attitude through humour when he paints an amusing portrait of a rich woman 'tottering' on her heels and walking 'unsteadily' across his 'carefully striped' lawn. This description suggests that her excessively high heels hamper her movements, making her seem comic. The gardener also refers to expensive possessions such as her 'brand new' car in order to highlight the irony of her claiming to have 'no cash'.

While readers may find Millais's description of his clients equally humorous, he gives the impression that he is not in the least amused. In his letter, anger seems to be seething close to the surface as he calls his models 'provoking' and refers to his own 'extreme passion'. However, like the gardener, he draws attention to aspects of his client's annoying behaviour such as the child screaming and struggling with 'successful obstinacy'.

The clients' own words feature in both texts as if the writers are using them to validate their negative attitudes. The rich woman speaks to the gardener in an authoritative tone, asking him to 'check the gutter outside the study window'. Here the gardener implies that she has no understanding of his role since she continues to issue orders even after he has explained that he doesn't 'really do that sort of thing'. Likewise, Millais lists some of the endearments the mother showers upon her son, such as 'Precious darling', which clearly contrast with his own critical opinion of the boy.

Both writers use repetition to highlight the irritations their clients cause them. The gardener writes, 'I stopped planting the wrong plant in the wrong spot that she had insisted upon'. Here his repetition of the adjective 'wrong' draws attention to the ridiculous nature of the client's instructions. Similarly, Millais repeats 'my' when the mother refers to her baby as 'my popsy' and 'my flower'. Millais then adds 'etc., etc.,' to the list to indicate that the mother continues gushing for even longer.

These men also reveal their attitudes by choosing their own names for their clients. The gardener refers to 'the Gardeners' World gardener', which allows him to convey a derogatory image of a man who knows a lot about plants but is not prepared to 'do the physical work'. Using a similar technique, Millais calls the dog and child 'these animals', implying that the child does not behave like a normal human being. He further reinforces this point by referring to the infant as 'it' in some instances.

The structure of both pieces suggests that the writers are seeking sympathy. Millais starts his letter by informing Mr Combe that his clients have caused him great anxiety. In contrast, the gardener gains sympathy indirectly through his anecdote about the rich lady client. Millais does something similar when he dedicates an entire paragraph to the horrors of working with the disobedient child. Having set up their first case studies, the gardener moves on to explain his attitude towards over-enthusiastic amateurs and Millais reveals the annoying traits of the child's mother.

Each writer suggests that their clients push them close to breaking point. The gardener gets 'very close to snapping' and Millais feels as if he could 'almost murder' the child. However, their use of 'close to' and 'almost' suggests that, in order to maintain clients, both writers had to keep their critical feelings in check.

In spite of these negative attitudes, the gardener refers to a rare 'dream client' who allows him to work without interference, while Millais admits that he finds the dog far easier than the child as 'I do more from this creature in a day than from the other in a week', showing that there are some more positive experiences with clients to be had.

Mid Level

The gardener shows us his attitude towards a rich lady client by creating a humorous description of her 'tottering' across the lawn. I think he is suggesting that she ruins the grass with her heels. He is clearly irritated because he also tells readers that she has a 'brand new car' but has not paid him for four weeks.

He also draws attention to the horrible way that this lady speaks to him. She treats him like some kind of servant. We are shown how she orders the gardener about and she tells him to 'check the gutter outside the study window'. The gardener has to explain 'that I was a landscape gardener and I didn't really do that sort of thing' but the woman takes absolutely no notice of him.

He is also annoyed by a kind of client that he calls a 'Gardener's World gardener'. This type of client thinks that he knows it all and stands right over the gardener all the time he is working. In this case the gardener gets 'very close to snapping', which may mean this type of client annoys him even more than the rich lady. He does, however, have some dream clients that it is a joy to work for but he calls these 'rare' so we know that he doesn't meet them often.

Millais is also annoyed by his clients but his tone seems angry and he feels an 'extreme passion' about them. Like the gardener he tells us how his clients behave to show us his attitude about them. He calls the child and the dog 'provoking', which means they annoy him. He also describes how the child struggles 'when forcibly held in its mother's arms'. I think he dislikes the mother as much as the child and he gets pretty upset when she puts the baby on its feet and allows it to 'displace everything'. She also won't agree to his suggestion that they should smack the child and then he wishes he could murder it.

Turn over for Question 5 answers

Paper 2: Section B

5 (AO5) (AO6)

Level	Skills descriptors
Higher	**Content (AO5)** Your writing is confidently matched to the purpose of the task. Your register is convincing and compelling to the audience. You use an extensive and ambitious vocabulary. Your work is well crafted. You make excellent use of linguistic devices. **Organisation (AO5)** Your writing is compelling. You make varied and inventive use of structural features. You include a range of convincing and complex ideas. Your paragraphs are linked fluently. **Technical Accuracy (AO6)** Your sentences are well defined and consistently accurate. You use a range of punctuation with a high level of accuracy. You use a full range of appropriate sentence forms for effect. You use Standard English consistently and appropriately. Your grammar is excellent. Your spelling is highly accurate, including the spelling of ambitious vocabulary.
Mid	**Content (AO5)** Your writing is generally well matched to the purpose of the task. Your register is generally matched to the audience. Your vocabulary is chosen for effect and you make some sophisticated word choices. You use linguistic devices successfully. **Organisation (AO5)** Your writing is engaging. You make effective use of structural features. You use a range of clear, connected ideas. Your paragraphs are well linked. **Technical Accuracy (AO6)** Your sentences are securely defined and mostly accurate. You use a range of punctuation, mostly with success. You use a variety of sentence forms for effect. You use Standard English appropriately. Your grammar is good. Your spelling is generally accurate, including the spelling of complex and irregular words.
Lower	**Content** (AO5) Your writing is sometimes matched to the purpose of the task. You try to match your register (level of formality) to the audience. You make an attempt to vary your vocabulary. You make some use of linguistic devices. **Organisation (AO5)** Some of your writing is clear. You use some structural features. You include a variety of linked and relevant ideas. You use paragraphs and make some use of discourse markers.

Lower (continued)	**Technical Accuracy (AO6)** Most of your sentences are correctly defined. You show some control of a range of punctuation. You try to use a variety of sentence forms. You mostly use Standard English. Some of your grammar is correct. Your work includes some accurate spelling of more complex words.

Sample student responses

Higher Level

Matched to purpose

Coherent structure

Use of figurative language

Appropriate use of contextual references

Dear Mr Dowling,

I was delighted to read Steven Malone's article advocating self-employment for young people in last week's edition of your paper. Thank you for appreciating the importance of this vital issue and for presenting it in such a positive light. From a teenage perspective, I can confirm that Mr Malone is right; his views clearly reflect my own.

One problem with the conventional job market is that it does not allow young people to use their talents. For many students, the years after their GCSEs are their best. Released from the necessity to study everything, they can follow their passions by signing up for college courses in Photography, Film Studies or Art. However, before the gilt has dried on their diplomas, all is lost, because the jobs they can get are not the ones they dreamed of. Imagine a talented artist stacking supermarket shelves or a would-be photographer serving your burger and chips.

I believe that finding the right job helps to build self-esteem. Work is about more than earning money; [Sophisticated use of a range of punctuation] *it is about establishing an identity.* That is why I agree that self-employment could be a great way forward for young people. Instead of slogging away for a pittance, they can use their real interests to transform the ugly duckling of the supermarket into the swan of success.

I appreciate that self-employment has its drawbacks. One of the biggest challenges in living the dream is funding it, but, for those who dare to fly free, help is at hand. A young person establishing their own business can apply for funding from government start-up schemes or the Prince's Trust. These options should reassure those who are holding back due to financial fears.

Use of anecdote

Ambitious vocabulary

Use of statistics

Use of a pattern of three and rhetorical questions

Each counter argument could have been dismissed individually here, e.g. how the funding prevents poverty, and how the meetings prevent social isolation

Consistently matched to purpose

While a big corporation can promise pensions, sick pay and security, we don't all want to work our way up from the bottom. Some of us thrive on the challenge of stepping out alone. When I was eight, I came up with my first business plan. I saved up my pocket money to buy twenty packets of soft mints so that I could sell them on to greedy or gullible school mates – for a profit, of course. Despite the fact that the headmaster confiscated the offending items and complained to my parents, that experience probably led to the entrepreneurial spirit that enthuses me today.

Having recently started my own Graphic Design business, I know most of the possible pitfalls of self-employment. Panicking parents is one of the greatest difficulties. Even though my family have always praised, encouraged and even actively displayed my creative efforts (that house I painted in year three is still stuck on the fridge door) they turned a whiter shade of pale when I finally suggested going freelance. Even when I proved I had done my homework by pointing out the 84% increase in self-employment since 2008, they asked countless questions: What about sick pay? Wouldn't I get lonely? Couldn't I be just as creative in my Aunt Patsy's poodle parlour?

Of course, I acknowledged these multiple objections and then swiftly switched focus. I swam my way straight into one of the aforementioned funding streams. I applied to the Prince's Trust, who agreed to fund my business. They also invited me to a series of informative (and very sociable) workshops, thereby alleviating my parent's fears about poverty and social isolation.

Now, I have created a brand, a website and a range of unique but affordable products. I'm even attending a basic accountancy course to help me complete tax returns (in spite of my terror of maths). Yes, anything is possible!

So thank you for publishing Mr Malone's article. Perhaps, as a result, somebody else will step through a window of opportunity just as I have done. I truly believe that self-employment is the 'best option' for young people. It allows them to follow their dreams, use their talents and have a lot of fun.

Yours sincerely,

Richard Payne

Mid Level

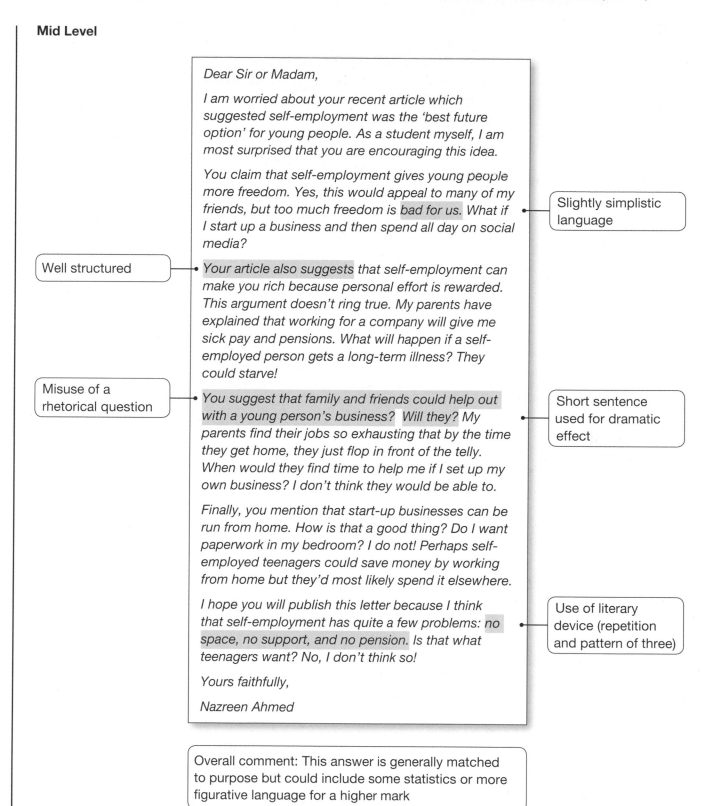

Dear Sir or Madam,

I am worried about your recent article which suggested self-employment was the 'best future option' for young people. As a student myself, I am most surprised that you are encouraging this idea.

You claim that self-employment gives young people more freedom. Yes, this would appeal to many of my friends, but too much freedom is bad for us. What if I start up a business and then spend all day on social media?

> Slightly simplistic language

Your article also suggests that self-employment can make you rich because personal effort is rewarded. This argument doesn't ring true. My parents have explained that working for a company will give me sick pay and pensions. What will happen if a self-employed person gets a long-term illness? They could starve!

> Well structured

You suggest that family and friends could help out with a young person's business? Will they? My parents find their jobs so exhausting that by the time they get home, they just flop in front of the telly. When would they find time to help me if I set up my own business? I don't think they would be able to.

> Misuse of a rhetorical question

> Short sentence used for dramatic effect

Finally, you mention that start-up businesses can be run from home. How is that a good thing? Do I want paperwork in my bedroom? I do not! Perhaps self-employed teenagers could save money by working from home but they'd most likely spend it elsewhere.

I hope you will publish this letter because I think that self-employment has quite a few problems: no space, no support, and no pension. Is that what teenagers want? No, I don't think so!

> Use of literary device (repetition and pattern of three)

Yours faithfully,

Nazreen Ahmed

Overall comment: This answer is generally matched to purpose but could include some statistics or more figurative language for a higher mark

Lower Level

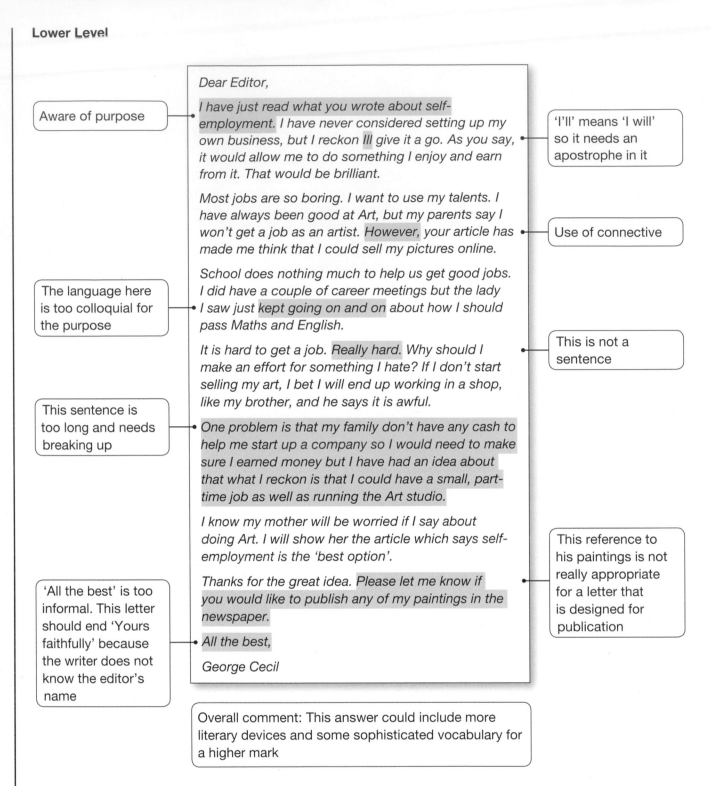

Aware of purpose

'I'll' means 'I will' so it needs an apostrophe in it

Use of connective

The language here is too colloquial for the purpose

This is not a sentence

This sentence is too long and needs breaking up

This reference to his paintings is not really appropriate for a letter that is designed for publication

'All the best' is too informal. This letter should end 'Yours faithfully' because the writer does not know the editor's name

Dear Editor,

I have just read what you wrote about self-employment. I have never considered setting up my own business, but I reckon Ill give it a go. As you say, it would allow me to do something I enjoy and earn from it. That would be brilliant.

Most jobs are so boring. I want to use my talents. I have always been good at Art, but my parents say I won't get a job as an artist. However, your article has made me think that I could sell my pictures online.

School does nothing much to help us get good jobs. I did have a couple of career meetings but the lady I saw just kept going on and on about how I should pass Maths and English.

It is hard to get a job. Really hard. Why should I make an effort for something I hate? If I don't start selling my art, I bet I will end up working in a shop, like my brother, and he says it is awful.

One problem is that my family don't have any cash to help me start up a company so I would need to make sure I earned money but I have had an idea about that what I reckon is that I could have a small, part-time job as well as running the Art studio.

I know my mother will be worried if I say about doing Art. I will show her the article which says self-employment is the 'best option'.

Thanks for the great idea. Please let me know if you would like to publish any of my paintings in the newspaper.

All the best,

George Cecil

Overall comment: This answer could include more literary devices and some sophisticated vocabulary for a higher mark